THE LIBRARY OF SOUTHERN CIVILIZATION
LEWIS P. SIMPSON, EDITOR

# THE INVISIBLE EMPIRE

# THE
# INVISIBLE EMPIRE

ALBION WINEGAR TOURGÉE

INTRODUCTION AND NOTES BY

OTTO H. OLSEN

LOUISIANA STATE UNIVERSITY PRESS
BATON ROUGE AND LONDON

New material copyright © 1989 by Louisiana State
  University Press
Manufactured in the United States of America
First printing

98 97 96 95 94 93 92 91 90 89   5 4 3 2 1

LIBRARY OF CONGRESS CATALOGING-IN-PUBLICATION DATA

Tourgée, Albion Winegar, 1838–1905.
    The invisible empire / Albion Winegar Tourgée ; introduction
and notes by Otto H. Olsen.
        p.    cm. — (The Library of Southern civilization)
    Reprint. Originally published as part II of an expanded
edition of the author's A fool's errand. New York : Fords,
Howard & Hubert, 1880.
    ISBN 0-8071-1462-6 (pbk. : alk. paper)
    1. Ku-Klux Klan.   I. Title.   II. Series.
HS2330.K63T6 1989
322.4′2′0973—dc19                                          88-28350
                                                                CIP

# CONTENTS

# INTRODUCTION

*The Invisible Empire,* by Albion Winegar Tourgée, first appeared in May, 1880, as Part II of an expanded edition of his Reconstruction classic *A Fool's Errand by One of the Fools.* That immensely popular novel, based upon Tourgée's experiences of fourteen years as a carpetbagger in North Carolina, had been published anonymously only six months earlier; and it was the announcement of a new edition of the novel, containing *The Invisible Empire* and available by subscription only, that ended Tourgée's anonymity as the author of *A Fool's Errand.*[1] The novel's new supplement was a work of nonfiction that depicted the activities of a variety of terrorist organizations operating in the South after the Civil War and commonly known as the Ku Klux Klan. It also provided a challenging analysis of racism and social conditions in the post–Civil War South.

At the time these works were published, the Radical Reconstruction effort had already been abandoned by the North, though that abandonment remained a matter of significant national debate. The informed and impassioned account of southern Reconstruction provided in 1879 by *A Fool's Errand* made that novel something of an immediate sensation; its stark depictions of violence and racist oppres-

---

1. Roy F. Dibble, *Albion W. Tourgée* (New York, 1921), 70–71.

sion aroused heated denials from the Democratic South and more than a little disbelief in the North. *The Invisible Empire* was a response intended to authenticate the historical accuracy of the novel by providing a factual account of Klan terrorism. Although the novel itself was substantially autobiographical, with its most dramatic incidents based upon fact, this was not generally appreciated at the time. Tourgée wanted to formalize the accuracy of his fictional portrayal and identify that portrayal with the Reconstruction South as a whole. Intentionally or not, Tourgée was following the path of Harriet Beecher Stowe, who had sought to legitimize her famous depiction of the slave South with the publication of *A Key to Uncle Tom's Cabin.*

For a variety of reasons, however, Tourgée's factual account of the Ku Klux Klan attracted almost no attention when it appeared. It was largely unnoticed by newspapers and journals, even including *Publishers Weekly,* and it was neglected by Tourgée's own publisher, Fords, Howard, & Hulbert. They had copies of the original novel to sell and almost invariably continued to advertise it without any mention whatsoever of the new edition containing *The Invisible Empire.*[2] The fact that this new edition was sold only by subscription probably also had an adverse effect on its fate. Subscription sales were perceived by some as an effort on the part of publishers to monopolize the market and avoid costs and commissions, and as such were a matter of public controversy at the time.[3] This sales method may have both encour-

---

2. For example, see advertisements from June, 1880, to June, 1881, in *Publishers Weekly,* XVII (January–June, 1880), 640; XVIII (July–December, 1880), 215, 310, 376; and XIX (January–June, 1881), 139, 356, 637. The only advertisement mentioning *The Invisible Empire* appeared on January 29, 1881, *ibid.,* XIX (January–June, 1881), 129.

3. *Publishers Weekly,* XIX (January–June, 1881), 548–50.

aged neglect by the booksellers and discouraged advertisement.

Several other factors were even more detrimental. *The Invisible Empire* was published only a few months after the initial appearance of the novel, and it was not issued as a separate volume. The very success of *A Fool's Errand* detracted attention from the new supplement, and because the original novel was still in the process of being reviewed, there was little or no interest in providing an immediate second review. Furthermore, history could not compete in the marketplace with fiction, especially when it was history that represented a rapidly fading point of view. Consequently, it was Tourgée's continuing promise as a novelist that monopolized attention in the world of books. While *The Invisible Empire* was ignored, Tourgée's progress in writing new fiction was reported on with some regularity, and as early as the summer of 1880, marked attention was focused upon his new Reconstruction novel, *Bricks Without Straw,* which proved to be another phenomenal success.[4]

One ironic consequence of the neglect of Tourgée's history of the Ku Klux Klan—a neglect that has continued to the present day—is that an additional chapter of *A Fool's Errand* itself has remained unnoticed. When the expanded edition of 1880 was published, the novel contained a new chapter, "Spring Buds and Sunshine," which, while not essential to the work, did add perceptive material on race relations and the freed population of the South.[5] That chapter has not been included in any of the reprints of *A Fool's Errand* except the

4. For discussions of Tourgée's writing, see *Publishers Weekly,* XVIII (July–December, 1880), 13, 164, 212–13, 310, 386, 413, 612, and XIX (January–June, 1881), 19, 488.

5. Originally the novel contained forty-seven chapters. In the expanded edition, the novel contained forty-eight chapters.

edition of 1902, and then it appeared only because that edition was a reprint of the original expanded edition of 1880.

Neglect of *The Invisible Empire* when it first appeared was particularly obvious in the publishing and literary world. The work was of somewhat greater interest to the political press, though only one full-scale review has been discovered. This was a very positive, two-column review that appeared in the New York *Tribune* on July 23, 1880. At that time, many Republicans, remembering the electoral crisis of 1876, were anxious to play down the issues associated with Reconstruction in a presidential election year. Not so the reviewer for the *Tribune*, who praised *The Invisible Empire* not only for establishing the facts about the Klan and confirming "the essential truthfulness and justice of the novel" but also for exposing the problem of continuing racist oppression in the South. Like Tourgée, the reviewer believed that the Reconstruction issues should be revived and the struggle continued until the promises of the Fourteenth and Fifteenth Amendments were fulfilled: "The midnight raiding by masked assassins has ceased; but it has ceased only because it has done its infamous work. 'With the suppression of the negro and Republican vote, and the establishment of minority rule, its purpose was accomplished. As a consequence, what is termed "peace" has succeeded to the reign of violence and terror. But it is the peace of force, of suppression, of subverted right, of trampled and defied law.' "[6] While this impatient Republican endorsed Tourgée's picture of the South, he considered the author's educational solution "at best a slow remedy." To the dominant white leaders of the South, on the other hand, Tourgée's purported exposure of the Klan was further cause for condemnation.

---

6. New York *Tribune*, July 23, 1880, p. 6.

In preparing his account of the Ku Klux Klan, Tourgée had an unusually convenient source of information in the transcript of a sweeping congressional investigation of southern violence that had been conducted in 1871. The testimony taken during that investigation covered most of the former Confederacy and was conveniently available in thirteen volumes published by the federal government.[7] *The Invisible Empire* was composed almost entirely from that source and consists primarily of excerpts from and an analysis of the firsthand testimony obtained from residents of Alabama and Georgia. Tourgée's presentation is reliable and sound, though what he designates as quotations are often paraphrased summaries rather than precise quotations from the congressional investigation. While such literary license is not in accord with professional historical methods, a careful check of Tourgée's paraphrasing shows that it is, almost without exception, accurate in its essence. The occasional instances in which this is not the case are indicated in the editor's notes to this reprint edition.

The testimony Tourgée utilized in his study was for many years discredited on the grounds that it consisted mainly of partisan views arranged by a Radical Republican Congress. The primary reason for this criticism, however, was that most of the evidence was at odds with historical attitudes prevailing in the United States from the end of Reconstruction up to the 1940s. Thus, while Tourgée retained the public's appreciation for the power and effectiveness of his fiction throughout his life, he was criticized for his historical

7. *Testimony Taken by the Joint Select Committee to Inquire into the Condition of Affairs in the Late Insurrectionary States* (13 vols; Washington, D.C., 1872). These volumes may be found as either *Senate Reports,* 42nd Cong., 2nd Sess., No. 41, or *House Reports,* 42nd Cong., 2nd Sess., No. 22.

bias, especially for failing "to show the horrors of the negro regime which made the Ku Klux Klan inevitable."[8]

Today the Ku Klux Klan is commonly perceived as one of the most nefarious forces in the history of the nation, but this perception has not always been prevalent. During Reconstruction, for example, the white South applauded the Klan as a defender of not only white supremacy but also home rule, honesty, good government, and, of all things, Christian morality, and law and order. And after northern whites abandoned their equalitarian Reconstruction commitments and subsequently embraced the age of segregation, they found it comforting to endorse negative assessments of the entire Reconstruction effort. With few exceptions, historians encouraged this sectional reconciliation by providing scholarly accounts that endorsed white supremacy and excused the activities of the Ku Klux Klan.

Tourgée's factual account was in direct conflict with this trend and was largely ignored by historians. Among early interpreters of the period, only Walter Lynwood Fleming specifically cited the work, and while he dismissed Tourgée's use of "worthless testimony from the Ku Klux Report," Fleming concluded that *The Invisible Empire* displayed "a very clear conception of the real meaning of the movement and a correct appreciation of its results." William Garrott Brown's work also appears to reflect Tourgée's analysis as well as his conclusion that public education was the only sensible solution to southern racial problems. More recently, Stanley Horn utilized the title and quoted from, but never specifically mentioned or cited, Tourgée's *The Invisible Empire*.[9] None of these historians endorsed Tourgée's

---

8. Obituary notice on Tourgée, in *Bookman*, XXI (1905), 458.
9. J. C. Lester and D. L. Wilson, *Ku Klux Klan: Its Origin, Growth and*

denunciation of the Klan or his equalitarian point of view.

Since the 1940s, a revolution has occurred in attitudes respecting Reconstruction, and that revolution has been marked by a steadily growing appreciation of Tourgée's conclusions. Just as the earlier commitment to racism helped initiate and maintain negative assessments of Reconstruction Republicanism, changing mores associated with a worldwide rejection of racism have inspired a contrasting view. Today the villains of Reconstruction are not the scalawags and carpetbaggers but the racist white Redeemers and their instrument of oppression, the Ku Klux Klan. This modern view has achieved full-scale expression in Allen W. Trelease's *White Terror: The Ku Klux Klan Conspiracy and Southern Reconstruction* and Wyn Craig Wade's *The Fiery Cross: The Ku Klux Klan in America*. Both authors cite *The Invisible Empire* and clearly endorse both the legitimacy of Tourgée's sources and the conclusions he reached.[10]

Different eras have thus differed drastically in their judgment of the Klan, but there have also been some substantial areas of agreement. Both old and new accounts have suggested that the development of the Klan into a significant

---

*Disbandment,* ed. Walter Lynwood Fleming (1905, rpr. New York, 1971), 18; William Garrott Brown, *The Lower South in American History* (New York, 1903), Ch. 4; Stanley F. Horn, *Invisible Empire: The Story of the Ku Klux Klan, 1866–1871* (1939; enlarged ed., Cos Cob, Conn., 1969). The quotation Horn attributes to Tourgée on page 28 is from Tourgée, *A Fool's Errand . . .* [and] *The Invisible Empire* (New York, 1880, 507 (p. 137 in this edition).

10. Trelease concludes: "By far the fullest and fairest discussion of the causes of the Ku Klux Klan then or later was the report of the Republican majority of [the] Congressional joint committee which investigated the Klan in 1871." Allen W. Trelease, *White Terror: The Ku Klux Klan Conspiracy and Southern Reconstruction* (New York, 1971), 429–30*n*96. The fullest bibliography on the Klan is Lenwood G. Davis and Janet L. Sims-Wood (comps.), *The Ku Klux Klan: A Bibliography* (Westwood, Conn., 1984).

social movement can be traced to the intense reaction of the
dominant white South to three things in particular: conquest
by the North, the impact of emancipation, and the imposition
of black suffrage. During the two years immediately following the war (1865–1867) and prior to the real rise of the Klan,
a persisting pattern of discrimination and violence against
assertive blacks and anti-Confederate whites was already
apparent in the South. But it was the imposition of black
suffrage in 1867 and the subsequent political success of the
southern Republican party that generated the widespread and
carefully organized reign of terror represented by the Ku
Klux Klan. This organized violence was largely, perhaps
even predominantly, racist in nature, but it was also much
more. It was a central part of the determination of those who
had traditionally dominated the South to restore self-rule and
destroy Reconstruction reforms and the southern Republican
party. Thus, Klan violence was particularly directed against
white and black Republican activists, and it served as a
means of restoring traditional rulers to power and defending
established property interests against the threat of democracy.

One of the fascinating things about the present-day at-
titude toward Reconstruction is the extent to which it con-
firms the judgment of southern Republicans of a century ago.
That no one appears to have been more rehabilitated than
Albion W. Tourgée is particularly appropriate, because
Tourgée's involvement in the Reconstruction drama extended far beyond his immediate role as a carpetbagger.

Reacting to the phenomenal success of *A Fool's Errand*
and the enduring hostility of the South to a carpetbagger and
his beliefs, Tourgée returned North in 1879 to pursue a new
career as a writer. He subsequently published such a substantial amount of fiction and nonfiction on Reconstruction and

the race question that he stands as the nation's most persistent and outspoken white champion of racial justice during the last decades of the nineteenth century. It was indicative of his impact that in the year of his death, 1905, William E. B. Du Bois's Afro-American Niagara movement sponsored a national memorial service for three "Friends of Freedom": William Lloyd Garrison, Frederick Douglass, and Albion W. Tourgée. A few years later the Niagara movement helped found the National Association for the Advancement of Colored People (NAACP), the kind of biracial civil rights organization that Tourgée had advocated for many years. The NAACP would, of course, achieve its greatest victory in the *Brown* decision of the United States Supreme Court in 1954. That decision repudiated segregation and the myth of "separate but equal" sanctified by the Court in the *Plessy* v. *Ferguson* decision of 1896. The chief counsel for Homer Adolph Plessy in that earlier unsuccessful court fight against Jim Crow had been Albion W. Tourgée, and what had been a defeat for him in 1896 became a posthumous victory in *Brown* v. *Board of Education* fifty-eight years later.

Tourgée's career and writings were also being reevaluated during this time.[11] A favorable reconsideration of his literary work was under way by the 1930s, and in 1961 a new edition of *A Fool's Errand* was published in the John Harvard Library Series, with an appreciative introduction by the prominent historian John Hope Franklin. The following year, Tourgée's merits were applauded in Edmund Wilson's influ-

11. The most complete bibliography on Tourgée is Marguerite Ealy and Sanford E. Marovitz, "Albion Winegar Tourgée (1838–1905)," *American Literary Realism*, VIII (1975), 53–80. The fullest biography is Otto H. Olsen, *Carpetbagger's Crusade: The Life of Albion Winegar Tourgée* (Baltimore, 1965).

ential *Patriotic Gore: Studies in the Literature of the American Civil War*. Since then there have been new editions of Tourgée's novels; a lengthy list of related articles, doctoral dissertations, and bibliographies; and two new biographies, one of which utilized Tourgée's career to substantially revise the history of North Carolina Reconstruction. Furthermore, it has become apparent that rather than simply being rehabilitated, Tourgée has played an important role in inspiring the changes that have occurred. In the Introduction to a 1966 edition of *A Fool's Errand*, George Fredrickson suggested the breadth of that role when he wrote that "the author of *A Fool's Errand* deserves our attention as an early and forceful advocate of civil rights for all Americans, and as a thoroughgoing exponent of democracy, a true believer who did not shy away from the hard choices which history requires of the faithful." More recently another historian, Terry Seip, concluded that "in many respects Tourgee is the spiritual father of much recent work on southern Republicanism."[12]

Despite this extensive rehabilitation of Tourgée and his work, the study published here has remained neglected. Since 1902 *The Invisible Empire* has been reprinted only one time, by Gregg Press in 1968, and unfortunately that reprint includes an introductory sketch that seriously misconstrues Tourgée and his work. Particularly egregious is the assertion that "*The Invisible Empire* was written as a condemnation of the South; its people and institutions; past and present, and gave no basis of hope in a better future."[13] On the contrary,

---

12. Albion W. Tourgée, *A Fool's Errand: A Novel of the South During Reconstruction,* ed. George Fredrickson (New York, 1966), xxv; Terry Seip, *The South Returns to Congress: Men, Economic Measures, and Intersectional Relationships, 1869–1879* (Baton Rouge, 1983), 271n4.

13. Introductory sketch, in Tourgée, *The Invisible Empire* (Ridgewood, N.J., 1968), n.p.

Tourgée specifically emphasized that his intent was not "to awaken hostility or inspire prejudice" against the South but to clarify the facts as a means of bringing about positive change. Furthermore, rather than offering no basis of hope, he vigorously pressed for a reasonable solution. His proposed solution was the initiation of a full-scale attack on southern illiteracy through a program of federal aid to education, and in defending such a program, Tourgée insisted that the North fully shared responsibility for conditions in the South.[14]

On the other hand, one can say that in this instance, Tourgée's analysis of racism focuses almost exclusively upon the racism of the South while neglecting that of the North. But he was, after all, writing about the South, where the overwhelming majority of Afro-Americans then lived. And it would be difficult to deny Tourgée's contention that there was something unusually virulent, widespread, and crucial about racism in the post–Civil War South. The essence of the matter was that Tourgée was resisting a national reconciliation based upon an abandonment of both southern blacks and equalitarian principles. He sought instead to promote democracy and sectional reconciliation by exposing, discrediting, and undermining racist oppression in the South. Unfortunately, the nation followed precisely the opposite tack and found its harmony in a reaffirmation of racist belief and practice on a national scale. Tourgée had no tolerance for such an accommodation.

The reprint that follows is a photo-offset copy of the original. Unfortunately, therefore, the word *Negro* has not been capitalized, though Tourgée himself fought his publishers for its proper capitalization. Notes have been added, pri-

14. In this reprint edition, see pp. 18–20, 146–51.

marily for purposes of identification, clarification, and historiographical explanation, and they are followed by a list of errata discovered in the original. Because *The Invisible Empire* was published as Part II of *A Fool's Errand,* the pagination of the original runs from page 385 through page 521. For convenience, the pages of this reprint have been renumbered. The reader will also find note numbers added in the margins of the text.

It is indeed unfortunate that Tourgée's account of the Ku Klux Klan has been so largely neglected. His is an important and useful study that provides not only important insight into the mind of a so-called carpetbagger but also an analysis of the Klan that is concise, perceptive, well written, eminently instructive, and remarkably up to date. Such cannot be said, however, of every instance in which this account ventures into a more general analysis of southern society and history.

# THE INVISIBLE EMPIRE

# THE INVISIBLE EMPIRE.

## CHAPTER 1.

### REASONS FOR THIS WORK.

PART I. of this work, called "A Fool's Errand," portrays in narrative form the experiences, feelings, thoughts, and conclusions of a Northern man resident at the South since the war.

Not only is the truthful intent and spirit of the tale manifest on every page, but it is a fact that the greater portion of the incidents of the narrative were actual occurrences, of which the author had either personal cognizance or authentic information. Perhaps never before in literature has an apparent romance linked together so many literal facts. Strange, almost incredible to a Northern reader, it is, in itself, a marked verification of the adage that truth is stranger than fiction. It has been well denominated "truth in the disguise of fiction," for the web of romantic incident—itself mainly true—is but the garb which truth assumes the better to perform her task. Its verity has been fully substantiated since publication by letters to the author from a large number of northern men resident in the South, clergymen, ladies who have been teachers of colored schools, colored men, Southern white men who have suffered for their opinions, repentant Ku-Klux, and in fact all ranks and classes who would naturally have intimate knowledge of the truth portrayed in that work, and also of the spirit which underlay the incidents depicted. Revealing as it does, however, a state of society utterly at variance with all notions derivable from the study of Northern life, the tale is to a certain degree incomprehensible to the Northern mind; so that, for a better understanding of the opinions, feelings, and modes of thought among the Southern people, opportunity should be afforded for studying somewhat more in detail the history of the period in question, and for ascertaining how much of it was accidental, and how much essential; how much temporary, and how much fundamental.

The purpose of Part II., then, is to present in a more concrete and specific form some *authenticated record of events* contemporaneous with the action of "A Fool's Errand." The precise cases are not repeated—unhappily there is no dearth of facts; but the similarities and analogies will be strikingly patent. These incidents will enable the reader to decide for himself as to the accuracy of the conclusions at which the author has arrived, and judge with greater certainty as to the remedy proposed.

It has been intimated by more than one reviewer that "it would be interesting to know where fact ended and fiction began" in the narrative of "A Fool's Errand;" and one has wondered "how wide a fringe of fancy surrounds the narrative of facts :" but the reader of the following pages will readily see that fact had no end and fiction no beginning in that narrative, so far as its incidents are concerned; imagination did but weave them together. Compared with the vast multitude of recorded incidents from which those were taken, the whole book, indeed, is but a "fringe"—not "of fancy," however, but of hard, unquestionable fact.

To fairly present in this form the history and spirit of the period referred to, is a task neither light nor grateful. It is onerous because of the superabundance of material from which selection must be made to bring the result within proper bounds, and unpleasant because in its performance many a kind and charitable illusion must be torn aside. The subject is one which every right-minded and right-hearted man must approach with something of reluctance, but which nevertheless

THE RISING GENERATION.

is a duty not to be shirked. The desire for national unity and concord—the very fact that republican government is felt by all to be yet upon its trial in our country—inclines every patriotic mind to wish that the problem of Reconstruction may at last be solved peacefully, and also justly and satisfactorily to all sections and classes. "Let us have peace" became the slogan of a great party, not merely because uttered by its chosen leader at the close of a terrible civil convulsion, and in the hour of victory achieved so largely through his efforts, but because it voiced the universal sentiment of the North with reference to its long separated and disturbed neighbor. Mingled with this sentiment was also a feeling of universal sympathy for the losses and troubles which the South had brought upon itself by the war for disunion; and this readily grew into a determination to think no evil of the enemy with whom there had been such recent reconciliation. It was the natural feeling which one has when a broken friendship has been renewed—a resolution never to allow it again to be ruptured, and also a determination to make no reference or allusion to the causes of former difference. This feeling, proper and beautiful as it is, has resulted in a willful blindness in regard to the period we are considering, which has prevented any careful analysis of its developments or appreciation of its spirit and motives by the people of the North. The feeling has been that these things were but dying embers of a great conflagration which a brief time and simple exposure to the natural elements would serve to extinguish.

Again, that period is thought to be too near to the present to be viewed with absolutely dispassionate coolness. The excitement of party conflicts, the sting of personal experience, the intensity of individual sentiment and conviction, must be thought to discredit, in greater or less degree, the efforts of any one who shall attempt such a task. Perhaps the preceding pages disclose as little of such feeling as is possible in any one writing at this time of what he has himself seen and known. Being, however, the views of one man, they very naturally arouse in the mind the question whether his views and experiences were not exceptional, and whether his conclusions are just and trustworthy. It is not only natural but it is highly proper that there should be a wish for further information upon this subject.

But there is something beyond the desire to test the truthfulness and justice of "A Fool's Errand," although its statements have aroused wide attention. What is known as the "Southern Question" is not by any means a settled or even a quiet one in these days. Despite the failure of Reconstruction, the collapse of the State governments founded on the votes of the entire people (including the newly-enfranchised race), the resumption of "the white man's government" of those States, and the return of white-winged peace to those communities lately distracted with midnight violence and riotous elections, there is evidently still some disturbing influence at work. The murmurs of discontent among a race which constitutes nearly one half the population of the South, whose situation and condition are entirely anomalous in history, have reached a point where they can no longer be hushed or disregarded. Even as these lines are written, the colored man, overleaping the traditions of the past, smothering the strong local attachments for which his race has always been remarkable, and braving the evils which ignorance and uncertainty must greatly magnify to his mind, is crowding the avenues to the great Northwest. The fact that the negro braved want and cold and danger and suffering to escape from slavery, was generally regarded in the *ante-bellum* days as a conclusive argument against the absolute beatitude of slavery as a state of society, and as affording reasonable ground for doubt in regard to the negro's incapacity to enjoy any other state of existence. During the past *year* more colored men have come to the North as refugees than ever came in *five years* during the days of slavery. Within a fortnight the writer of these lines has seen one party of more than a hundred, coming from four different States of the South, without preconcert or knowledge of each other's movements, all seeking a home upon the plains of Kansas, and all giving as a reason for their action a desire to go where their children may grow up as freemen.  At this moment a committee of the United States Senate is engaged in investigating the causes, character and consequences of this movement as affects one state to which they are tending.  It will be seen therefore that the question as to what motives animate and control the different classes of the South—how much of the spirit of slavery and its incidents still exists—is one of *present* interest and importance to the whole Nation.

That Reconstruction failed entirely to achieve the objects which it was intended to secure, is a fact so patent as to go without denial; whether any other feasible plan would have accomplished better results is, at the best, but an interesting historical question: but what now remains to be done, whether by the Nation, by the separate States, or by the moral sentiment and action of individuals, is a question of prime importance to every citizen of whatever race or section.  That the Nation is not homogeneous; that the motive, spirit, and sentiment of one section are hostile and obnoxious to those of another, no man can deny.  Whether the two be termed a " Northern civilization" and a " Southern civilization," or one be called a "civilization" and the other "a lack of civilization," is a mere matter of verbal taste.  The fact remains that there *is* a difference between the fundamental feelings and principles of the North and those of the South.  The interests of good government, prosperity, and peace demand that these differing spirits should be harmonized as soon as may be.

The first essential to the cure of an evil is to understand its character.  The first act of a skillful physician is to make a diagnosis—to discover the extent and nature of the disease he has to treat.  The mere claim that this unpleasant matter is over, has been settled, and ought to be let alone, will accomplish nothing.  *Is* it over ?  *Has* it been settled ?

A man was wounded in battle.  The ball was extracted, the wound healed, and he went again to duty.  Ten years afterwards his health failed, and a surgeon investigating the cause of disease said, "It is this wound."  "But," it was objected, "that is healed.  There is no more inflammation; no more suppuration.  All that is left is a mere scar."  "Ah!" was the reply, "so it seems, but underneath that scar is a portion of the missile which caused it."  An operation was performed, and a fragment was found which was steadily eating its way to a vital part.  It was, no doubt, an unpleasant course to adopt, but it was nevertheless a wise one.  The extirpation of evil is never accomplished without pain.  There is no anesthetic that can be applied to the body politic, by which a diseased nation may pass into a dreamless sleep and awake healed and in its right mind.  Under the half-healed scars of the past are hidden malign influences which are even now threatening the Nation's peace and prosperity.  Must they, then, be let alone?

He who would reopen the wounds of the past merely to awaken sectionalism, "party spirit," and hate, to call forth evil passions which have been consigned to the silent care of a dead past, is worthy only of unmeasured execration.  But, to comprehend the spirit and condition of the South to-day, we must have constantly in mind both its recent and remote history; we must recognize and understand the influences which have for generations acted upon the minds and hearts of its people.  In other words, we must, as a people, diagnose the evil which threatens the body politic, if we would apply a remedy which shall be reasonable, safe, and efficacious.

This is the principle which has been steadily kept in view in the former part of this work.  The endeavor has there been made to present and illustrate, in narrative form, the state of society at the South during the reconstructionary era, so far as regards the *spirit of different classes towards each other and the Nation;* and also to analyze and dissect—so as to present them in a simple and comprehensible form to the reader—the causes which led up to these feelings and secured these results.  The same object will be pursued in the remaining pages, the purpose of which is only to give some authenticated illustrations of the facts already recited, the causes leading to them, and the remedy suggested for them.

## CHAPTER II.

### THE METHOD OF INQUIRY.

IN considering the actual condition of the South, it should be remembered that with the Southern people political prejudice is the strongest possible passion which can be aroused, and that such prejudice has very naturally been at fever-heat since the close of the war.

It should also be remembered that the orators and writers of the South have, with rare exceptions, been all upon one side of the political controversies of the day. Four-fifths of the whites of the South— -in many sections nine-tenths, and not unfrequently a greater proportion of them—have been solidly arrayed against the remainder of their own race and the colored people. The white Republicans of the South must be rated below the average of their fellow-citizens in respect to wealth and intelligence, and especially in the matter of property. It is not probable that at any time more than one-fifth of the education and wealth of the South was held by Republicans. The press was almost entirely in the hands of the Democrats because a Republican press had small means of existence. To the class that tried to accept the new order of things, therefore, the power of utterance, the capacity for that continuous reiteration of facts which finally dins them into the public ear and fastens them upon the public conscience, was almost entirely denied. The press of the South is not representative of them, their thoughts, experiences, and desires, and indeed has never claimed to be. From the first it has declared itself to be the champion and representative of the "white people of the South," meaning that portion of the white race which did not coöperate politically with the blacks. It is consequently of little use to turn to their columns for testimony upon this

subject, though we may notice some unconscious revelations
which are startling in their character.

The great reservoir of undigested facts pertinent to this matter is the Report of the Joint Congressional Committee on the
Ku-Klux Conspiracy, embracing thirteen closely printed octavo
volumes, containing more than six thousand large pages, or the
equivalent of *twenty-five thousand of the pages of this book.*

This exhaustless store of evidence is the result of an inquiry
which was concluded in 1872, and was chiefly concerned with
the events of the previous four years.

Just here it may be well to state a fact which has generally
escaped the memory of Northern men who have not been especially concerned in political life, viz. : that the first State governments which went into operation under the Reconstruction
Acts of Congress were organized about the first of July, 1868.
Before that time the Johnsonian Provisional Governments were
in operation, while the commanders of the various Military
Districts had supervisory and discretionary power to modify or
set aside their acts when deemed by them unjust and oppress-
ive.   During this time there was, in effect, but one party at
the South.   The colored men had not then been admitted to
the right of suffrage, and the old property qualifications in sev-.
eral of the States still applied to the white voters.   The power
of these Provisional Governments was solely in the hands of
the majority of white voters, while the representation in the
legislatures was based on population; the Union element of
those States thus being in a minority so hopeless as to render
it powerless for good or evil.   Whatever struggle there was at
the ballot-box was entirely local in its character, and almost
always between individuals of varying shades of the same political faith.   The administration of government and the enforcement of law during this time was lodged in the magistracy
and officers appointed by these Provisional Governments, except in the few instances where they were superseded by ap-
pointees of the military commanders of the respective districts.

The Republican party was first organized in the South in the
spring and summer of 1867 (just two years after the close of

the war), and colored men first voted under the Reconstruction
Acts at the elections held for delegates to Constitutional Conventions in the several States in the fall of that year.

Thus, it will be seen that the negro did not become a potential factor in Southern politics until the fall of 1867, and that
no governments were organized through his influence or under
Republican auspices until the midsummer of 1868. These
facts will be found to be of prime importance in considering
the matters which will be laid before the reader, since they give
a key, otherwise difficult to obtain, to the motive and spirit of
the actors in the scenes of violence which marked these years
and in various forms have continued until the present. Every
reader should therefore fix in his mind at the outset these three
points:

1. From the Surrender, in April, 1865, until July, 1868, the
Provisional or Johnsonian State Governments existed at the
South, with supervisory power in the commander of the Milita-
ry District after the spring of 1867.

2. The Republican party was organized at the South in the
spring of 1867, and colored men first voted in the fall of that
year.

• 3. The first Reconstructionary Governments were organized,
and the States readmitted under them, in July, 1868.                4

With these preliminary facts well in mind, we will go forward upon our path of inquiry. And if it seems to be a limit-
ed one, confined to the disclosure of a single line of development—the history, in fact, of the Ku-Klux organization—the
reader will remember that this immense and efficient enginery,
which in a few months overspread a territory larger than modern Europe, powerful enough to cope with a nation of conquer-
ors, and exact enough to catch and grind to powder the most
insignificant individual obnoxious to its hate, was the organic representative of the ideas, the sentiments, the intentions,
and the determination of "the South." It is to be studied as
an authenticated type, a recognized exponent.

The vast volume of the testimony taken by the Congressional
Committee referred to, as well as the fact that their report

proper presented no adequate summary or analysis of its character (as indeed it would be nearly impossible to do within the
compass of such a report), has prevented the facts appearing
therein from becoming generally known. Besides that, the
nation had supped full of horrors in the decade of civil strife
which it had just passed through, and the public mind was
anxious to escape the consideration of such apparently remedi-
less evils. It is none of our present purpose to attempt to summarize the entire contents of those volumes, but only to present
extracts from the testimony which may serve to further illustrate and substantiate the narrative presented in the first part
of this volume, and to give some reasonable analysis of the underlying spirit, motive, and—so to speak—principle, that moved
half a million men to these deeds of savagery. These instances,
the striking similarity of many of which to the incidents already narrated will be noted at once, are taken chiefly from
those volumes of the Report which embrace the inquiry relating
to the States of Georgia and Alabama. They are but samples
even of those, culled almost at random from pages overloaded
with like testimony. They are but isolated cries which come
up from a few individuals out of the thousands who lay strick-
en on the field where the hostile "civilizations" met in silent ˙
and unnoted but yet woeful conflict. These States are selected
because they have usually been accounted as among the more
peaceful. They have witnessed no wholesale slaughters like
those of New Orleans and Memphis, of Hamburg and Ellenton.
But the motive power is everywhere the same, and the few cita-
tions here made will suffice to show the spirit, causes, and consequences of these acts, and direct the mind of every honest-
minded citizen to the consideration of the remedy already suggested, as the true and only cure for the ills delineated.

In every instance the name of the witness and the volume
and page on which his testimony may be found will be given,
and in most cases also a brief statement of his standing and
antecedents. The purpose is to invite scrutiny and awaken
thought, and not to present argument or engage in controversy. The past is dead. Its acts are buried. The late Reverdy

Johnson, when appearing as counsel for certain of the perpetrators, horrified by the testimony adduced in the course of the
trial, threw up his hands and exclaimed: "It is simple savagery, for which there can be no excuse or palliation." We
may echo this candid cry; and yet it would be an act of ghoul-
ish horror to drag these things again to the light of day, were
it not that the spirit which prompted, permitted, and excused
such acts is but a part of that development which is termed
"Southern civilization," and the effects of which are everywhere to be seen. As such, it constitutes a part of the present,
and typifies a spirit which may at any moment burst forth
afresh in the future.

The opinion has been ventured in "A Fool's Errand" that
only GENERAL EDUCATION—*universal enlightenment of
whites and blacks alike*—can be relied upon to change the spirit
which moved these horrors, and that it is the first great duty
of the Nation to provide for such enlightenment. How this
may be done, is a question for further consideration; but that
it must be done, the history of freedom and Christian civilization as contrasted with this record leaves little in doubt. We
ask any reader to consider the pages which follow and then
deny that doctrine if he can—if he dare!

## CHAPTER III.

### RISE, SCOPE, AND PURPOSE OF THE KU-KLUX KLAN.

REFERRING to "A Fool's Errand," from page 170 onwards, and especially pages 244 to 252, for a general description of the rise of organized terrorism in the South, let us examine it more specifically. "THE KU-KLUX," as a generic term, embraced the various orders of "The Constitutional Union Guards," "The White Brotherhood," "The Society of the Pale Faces," "The Knights of the White Camelia," "The Invisible Empire," and an order the name of which was represented in their printed documents only by stars, which Gen. N. B. Forrest and other members declared had no name. Whether these various orders were different degrees of one organization, or were merely different names for the same thing in different localities, it is impossible to say. It would seem, from all that has become known, that the "Invisible Empire" was a higher grade, a more important and thoroughly guarded degree than the others—a ruling, controlling, and select circle, within and above the more numerous and popular grades of the order. It is a somewhat peculiar fact that though the signs, passwords, and general methods of procedure of the other branches of the Ku-Klux organizations were obtained from many sources, the information in regard to this was very scanty and unsatisfactory. A few admitted themselves to be members of it, but little if anything has ever been learned in regard to its organization and plan of operations. It was known to be an existent fact all over the South, and was generally believed by the members of the other kindred orders to be the directing and controlling central circle of them all.

This view is greatly strengthened by the fact that they all seem to have had a common origin, and all who speak with regard to the report in reference to its source accord the credit of its institution and supreme headship to Gen. N. B. Forrest, the noted Confederate cavalry general and the ill-famed hero of the massacre of Fort Pillow.                                6

From his own testimony, it appears that the order was first instituted in Tennessee during the year 1866, though it does not seem to have extended much beyond that State or to have attracted general public attention until about the first of 1868. In January, 1868, so far as appears, the name *Ku-Klux Klan* first became a part of our printed vocabulary. In February of that year, the newspapers of the North began to herald its doings through the country as a huge joke which certain pretended ghostly night-riders were playing upon the ignorant freedmen of the South, making them believe that they were the spirits of slain Confederates hailing from hell and slain in some great battle, which was almost always Shiloh, a fact which in itself marks the South-Western origin of the invention. At this time the illustrated newspapers began to teem with caricatures of the disguised horsemen and frightened darkies; and the peculiar *clucks* which were used by them as a signal, and from which the organization has taken its best-known name, became familiar about this time to the street Arabs of the Northern cities. The country regarded it as a broad farce, 7 not by any means accepting the old apothegm that "one might as well be killed as scared to death." It was thought to be a very pleasant and innocent amusement for the chivalry of the South to play upon the superstitious fears of the recently emancipated colored people. The nation held its sides with laughter, and the Ku-Klux took heart from these cheerful echoes and extended their borders without delay. It must be stated here, however, in palliation of this conduct of the North, that the previous murders and outrages by organized bands in Tennessee, reported by that wisest and noblest of our soldiers, Gen. Geo. H. Thomas, were not then known to have been com- 8 mitted by these men, and were not connected in the minds of the laughers with the grotesque uniforms of the Klan.

Between January and May of 1868, General Forrest seems to

have visited nearly all of the Southern States, and immediately after his visit in each State there was a sudden and widespread reign of Ku-Klux horrors.   He was in Georgia in February, and in North Carolina in March, 1868; both of which periods are fixed by the testimony as the dates on which the Ku-Klux was first heard of in those regions.

9          WALTER BROCK, a lawyer and farmer of Haralson County, Ga., native of Arkansas and forty-three years old, giving a conversation with one Daniel Dodson, a confessed Ku-Klux, says :

"He told me that Wm. Pond commanded the den, but they had recently turned him out and put in another : he did not know who he was.   He said they had each to pay his dollar, initiation-fee or something of that sort, and they paid it, and Billy failed to account for it to General Forrest, and they turned him out.   .   .   .   He told me that Gen. Forrest was the chief of the order."   (*Reports*, Vol. 7: pp. 1012–1017.)

The first operation on the part of the Ku-Klux in Georgia was the killing of Senator Ashburn at Columbus, on the 31st of

10        March, 1868.   Rev. J. H. Caldwell, native of South Carolina, and Judge of the District Court for the 37th senatorial district of Georgia, testifies :

"Q.—Did you see any prominent person here from a neighboring State, about that time, who had been publicly rumored to be a prominent officer of the order ?

"A.—Yes, sir; several—one in particular.   .   .   .   General Forrest.   .   .   .   I saw him and was introduced to him about the close of the convention, which adjourned on the 11th of March."   (Vol. 6: pp. 432–433.)

Many other witnesses testify to the same general report. Gen. Forrest, in his own testimony, is careful not to deny such report, but tries to leave the inference that what he knew of the order was merely incidental.   He says, however :

"I was getting at that time from one hundred to one hundred and fifty letters a day, and had a private secretary writing all the time.   I was receiving letters from all over the Southern States, men complaining, whose friends had been killed or families insulted and they were writing to me to know what they ought to do."   (Vol. 13: p. 9.)

This would be a very natural thing, if he were the "Grand Wizard of the Empire" (mentioned in the very interesting

"Prescript" or constitution of the order, annexed to his testimony and beginning on page 35 of Vol. 13), whose duties are described in Art. IV as follows :

"DUTIES OF OFFICERS. *Grand Wizard.* Art. IV., Sec. 1. It shall be the duty of the Grand Wizard, who is the supreme officer of the empire, to communicate with and receive reports from the Grand Dragons of Realms as to the condition, strength, efficiency, and progress of the *s within their respective realms ; and he shall communicate from time to time to all subordinate *s through the Grand Dragons the condition, strength, efficiency and progress of the *s throughout his vast empire, and such other information as he may deem expedient to impart. And it shall further be his duty to keep by his G. Scribe a list of the names (without any caption or explanation whatever) of the Grand Dragons of the different realms of his empire, and shall number such realms with the Arabic numerals, 1, 2, 3, &c., *ad finem.* And he shall instruct his Grand Exchequer as to the appropriation and disbursement which he shall make of the revenue of the *s that comes to his hands. He shall have the sole power to issue copies of this Prescript, through his subalterns and deputies, for the organization and establishment of subordinate *s. And he shall have the further power to appoint his Genii, also a Grand Scribe and a Grand Exchequer for his department, and to appoint and ordain Special Deputy Grand Wizards to assist him in the more rapid and effectual dissemination and establishment of *s throughout his Empire. He is further empowered to appoint and instruct deputies to organize and control realms, dominions, provinces, and dens, until the same shall elect a Grand Dragon, a Grand Titan, a Grand Giant, and a Grand Cyclops, in the manner hereinafter provided."

It is strongly in confirmation of Forrest's connection with the order, that that officer upon cross-examination was quite *unable to remember the name of his secretary*, did not know where he then was, and had not heard of him in eighteen months. However, with the amount of correspondence Gen. Forrest had on hand we may very well rely upon his statement in a letter under date of September 3d, 1868, as to the extent of the order.

Said he, "It was reported, and I believed the report, that there are *forty thousand* Ku-Klux in Tennessee ; and I believe the organization stronger in other States." (Vol. 13: p. 35.)

Many witnesses testify to the numbers in the different States as reported by members of the band, all agreeing in the main with the above estimate. When the bill for amnesty to all who had been guilty of Ku-Klux outrages was before the Legislature of North Carolina in 1873, it was openly admitted and urged as an argument in favor of the passage of the bill that there were "from thirty to forty thousand members of the Klan" in that State. The general belief was that there were not less than *five hundred thousand* in the entire South. This belief is fully sustained by Gen. Forrest's estimate, which there is no doubt he stood in a position to make very accurate.

With the foregoing ideas as to the origin of this formidable "Empire," the vast area of territory it controlled and the magnificent army that served its behests, we naturally ask what was the impelling cause of this effort, and what the practical end to be gained by it.

There are several modes of getting a clear idea as to the aims of the organization. It is evident that no one motive was at the bottom of it, except the very broad and general one of an organized hostility to the elevation of the colored race, and, by consequence, to any and all things that might contribute to that—the Reconstruction Acts, negro suffrage, colored schools, Northern immigration with its revolutionary and "radical" ideas, and so on.

One of the plainest and most probable accounts of how and why the spread of this organization was welcomed by Southern men, of the better as well as of the lower grades, may be found in the testimony given before the committee by the Rev. A. S. Lakin, who was in 1867 appointed by Archbishop Clark to go on traveling commission as Presiding Elder of the M. E. Church, in Montgomery District of Alabama, taking the names of Presiding Elders and preachers, with the amounts of money due to each, as their reports had been obstructed, drafts abstracted, and preachers were suffering. He traveled 650 miles throughout Northern Alabama in the saddle.

"In my travels," he says, "I put up with some of the leading men of the State, and learned from them this fact: that they never would submit; that they never would yield; they had lost their property, their reputation; and, last and worst of all, their slaves were made their equals, or were likely to be, and perhaps their superiors, to rule over them.   In extended conversations with them I inquired how we would help ourselves.   They said there was an organization, already very extensive and that would spread over the Southern States, that would rid them of this terrible calamity.   I stated that we would be arrested and punished ; that the government would visit upon us probably heavier punishments than any we had experienced.   They said they could rule that and control it. I asked how, and they replied, 'Why, suppose a man drops out here '—meaning that they would kill him; 'while that is being investigated, another will drop out here, and there, and yonder, until the cases are so frequent and numerous that we will overwhelm the courts, and nothing can withstand the omnipotence of popular sentiment and public opinion.'   I gathered these facts from various sources; they seemed to be patent. On my arrival at Huntsville, after this long and tedious tour, I learned of the organization of the Ku-Klux Klan.   It answered precisely the description and seemed to answer precisely the design expressed by these leading men." (Vol. 8: pp. 111–112.)

## CHAPTER IV.

### THE SPIRIT OF THE THING.

THE acts of violence and outrage at the South after 1865 and before the inauguration of the State governments under the Reconstruction laws in 1868 have generally been lost sight of in estimating the character and spirit of the Ku-Klux organization, it having been generally accepted as a fact that this organization was but a counter-move inspired by the misgovernment which undoubtedly followed the ill-regulated results of Reconstruction.

It will be remembered that on May 29, 1865, President Johnson issued an amnesty proclamation, offering pardon to all who had been engaged in rebellion (except certain specified classes who had held offices in the cause of the Rebellion), on condition of taking an oath of allegiance to the United States; and in that same year the 13th Amendment to the Constitution, by which Slavery was to be forever abolished throughout the Union, was proposed by Congress and ratified by three-fourths of the then represented States.

On April 9, 1866, Congress passed, over President Johnson's veto, the Civil Rights Bill, protecting the Freedmen in their new position.

*During* 1866 *the " Invisible Empire" was organized in Tennessee.*

Throughout 1866-7 the contest between President Johnson and Congress concerning the mode of reconstructing the Union by the reception of the "seceded" States waxed hot; the President thinking it sufficient for those States to repeal their ordinances of secession, repudiate the Confederate debt, and ratify the 13th Amendment; Congress deeming it important, in addition, to secure the Freedman a fair chance as a citizen. Congress consequently passed the Reconstruction Acts in March,

1867, and proposed the 14th Amendment to the Constitution. This declared all persons born or naturalized in the United States to be citizens of the United States and of the State wherein they reside (thereby, of course, clothing the Freedmen   12 with the right to vote); apportioning Congressional representation among the several States according to the numbers of their whole population (thus giving the blacks full representation, in the choice of which they had a voice, instead of the three-fifths representation accorded before the war to the slave population, the choice of which rested with the whites alone); prohibiting the abridgment of the privileges of citizenship or deprivation of life, liberty or property without due process of law; reducing the representation of any State in the proportion in which the right to vote should be denied to any of its male inhabitants (thus making it the *interest* of the States to use the full negro vote); forbidding official station to any who had already violated their oath of allegiance to the constitution of the United States; and, finally, establishing the validity of the public debt of the United States, and prohibiting the payment of the debts incurred in aid of the Rebellion.

It is important to recall just what these Amendments were.

It was not until the summer of 1868 that the State Governments (except that of Tennessee) were organized under the Reconstruction Acts; on the 4th of July, 1868, the President   13 granted unconditional pardon to all who were not at that time under indictment for treason; and on the 18th of July, 1868, the 14th Amendment was declared ratified by all the States, the seceded States under their Provisional Governors having elected Conventions, adopted the 13th and 14th Amendments, and been restored to their relations with the Union, their Senators and Representatives being admitted to their seats in Congress.

The date of the proved commencement of General Forrest's organization of the "Rebel" against the "Union" element of Tennessee shows that its inception was aroused by the adoption of the 13*th Amendment abolishing slavery by the organic law of the land.* And here we may quote the succinct language of the

report of the Congressional Committee on the rise and the
after spread of the Ku-Klux Klan:

"Coming into existence after the thirteenth amendment to
the constitution was adopted, it visited its vengeance in Tennessee upon the negro and the Union man whose acts had lib-
erated him.  The Reconstruction acts, being another step to
secure national safety, were met with increased bitterness; and
the report of the committee of the Tennessee Legislature tells
the results in that, the then (1867–68) only Reconstructed State.
When the fourteenth amendment was proposed, conferring
citizenship and its rights and privileges upon the negro, and
imposing disabilities to hold office upon those who had already
disregarded the obligations of office, the contest became still
more bitter and more widely spread; and the spirit of the early
Tennessee organization is readily discerned in the atrocities
narrated by the reports of commanding officers and of the su-
perintendents of the Freedmen's Bureau and in the contested
election cases of 1868."

14

We may then, with midsummer of 1868 fixed as the *beginning*
of the Reconstructed Governments, and before they had been
proven either good or evil, glance for a moment at the state of
affairs in the South under the previous Johnsonian Provisional
Governments, and the administration of the Generals commanding the Military Districts of the South during that time.  The
claim of misgovernment, cruelty and oppression has, it is true,
been vociferously made against these officers, but the country
will be very loth at this time to believe such charges against
such soldiers as Generals George H. Thomas, Canby, J. J. Reynolds, Sheridan, Terry, and their able and honorable subordi-
nates.  We will summarize a few of the facts as officially cer-
tified:

General Hatch, then Assistant Commissioner of the Freedmen's Bureau, reported the following outrages to the Bureau
in the State of Louisiana during the *first nine months* of
1868:—Killed, 297; wounded by gunshot, 50; maltreated, 142
—Total, 489.

A Committee of the House of Representatives, investigating the same State during same period, find in addition the
following: — Killed, 784; wounded by gunshot, 50; maltreated, 365.  Appendix: Killed, wounded and maltreated,
164.  Total, in both reports, 1852,

15

The reports of the military commanders and officers of the Bureau in nearly all the other States show increasing acts of violence through 1867, and the undeniable extension of the organization of the Klan early in 1868. Says General Thomas in his report: "With the close of the last year (1867) and the beginning of the new (1868), the State of Tennessee was disturbed by the operations of a mysterious organization known as the Ku-Klux Klan. . . . Within a few weeks it spread over a great part of the State." Says General Reynolds, of the same time: "Armed organizations known as the Ku-Klux Klan exist in many parts of Texas, but are most bold and aggressive east of the Trinity River." Says General Terry, in command of Georgia: "There can be no doubt of the existence of numerous insurrectionary organizations known as Ku-Klux Klans, who, shielded by their disguise, by the secrecy of their movements, and the terror they inspire, commit crime with impunity." Of Alabama he says: "From Southern Alabama I learn of no trouble. The middle and northern parts of the State are, however, in a very insecure condition."                                                           16

These facts are cited merely to call to mind that the Klan had begun its operations and become fairly started on its career of crime *before* what are termed "Carpet-Bag governments," or governments under the Reconstruction Acts, had been organized or had opportunity to display any mismanagement or corruption—while the States were still Military Districts, having Provisional Governments under the Johnsonian plan.

The causes from which Ku-Kluxism arose are almost as numerous and complex as the excuses which have been offered for its existence and its acts. The volumes comprising the Report of what is known as the Ku-Klux Committee, present in themselves a queer commentary upon the legislation connected with the Reconstruction Era. So far as the Committee was concerned, its career was a battle-royal between the most skillful champions of two great political parties. The motive of the majority evidently was to fasten the responsibility for these outrages upon the Democratic party, and the purpose of the minority was as evidently to establish a non-political character for the outrages and the organization that committed them, and also, as a counter-foil and excuse, to establish incapacity and misgovernment upon the part of the Reconstructionary Republican State organizations. Between these two ideas, *the condition of the poor victims themselves,* and the apparent hopelessness of good governments in communities where such barbarities were possible under any state of facts, seems to have been largely overlooked. But for the then impending struggle between the two opposing parties for the Presidency at the election of 1872, it is by no means probable that we should have had this inexhaustible store-house of facts, which to the student of social science, the historian, the economist, and the earnest-minded patriot offers lessons that they will seek in vain to learn from other sources, unless indeed they have been taught in the harsh and ungrateful school of experience. Directly or indirectly it lays open the inmost recesses of the Southern heart for the cool and, it is to be hoped, always charitable inspection of the world.

The witnesses consist of four classes:

1.—Victims of Ku-Klux violence and witnesses of it.

2.—Sympathizers with the victims.

3.—Ku-Klux—members or former members of the Klan.

4.—Sympathizers with Ku-Klux, or those who were inclined to abet or palliate their offences.

The unconscious and in many cases unintended testimony of each of these classes not unfrequently tells more than their studied and deliberate statements. The following facts may be taken as established beyond controversy. Indeed, they cannot be said to have been seriously denied—being denied, if at all, by a mere negation of knowledge on the part of the witnesses :

1.—The existence and almost simultaneous organization of the Klan in every one of the Southern States.

2.—The actual perpetration of the thousands of acts of violence testified to by the various witnesses. In relation to these facts there was absolutely no conflict of testimony. That the murders and whippings and mutilations were incontrovertible facts, was admitted by all.   Only the *motive* of the acts was put in controversy.

3.—That the Ku-Klux Klan was composed entirely of *white* men, who were opposed to the political equality of the colored man and to those of the whites who acted with him politically.

4.—That the outrages bore a striking similarity to each other throughout the whole field of inquiry:—were perpetrated by disguised bands in the night-time, in gangs varying from ten or twelve to two or three hundred ; that these bodies seemed always to be under the command of a recognized leader, were in good disciplinary subjection, always claimed to be part of a great organization, and almost invariably appeared to be engaged in the performance of a deliberately planned and specified task.   In almost all cases the parties were mounted, and usually upon good horses—a fact which of itself shows them to have had the co-operation and approval of the better classes throughout the South, since the poor men of the South, as a rule, cannot afford to ride horseback.   Whatever organization appears mounted on good horses in the country districts of the South must of necessity be composed of the much boasted "best citizens," or by those who represent them with their approval.   There is no doubt but the law which permitted "substitutes" in the Confederate army was held to justify a similar course in regard to the actual rank and file of the Ku-Klux Klan.

5.—That the victims of these outrages in almost every case belonged to one of the following classes :—(*a.*) Colored men ; (*b.*) White men who acted with the blacks politically ; (*c.*) Renegade members of the Ku-Klux Klan, or of the Democratic party.

These and other admitted facts are sufficient to fix the extent and general character of the organization and make conclusive the fact that the best and highest classes of the South did participate in, aid, and abet the movement.   There, more than anywhere else in the country, the influence of leading men and first families is most potent, for good or evil.   The claim that poor rough outcasts of society and the like discreditable characters are responsible for this besom of bloody vengeance that swept from the shores of the James to the waters of the Rio Grande is of all things most absurd to one who knows from experience the constitution of Southern society, or who will thoughtfully consider the patent facts of Southern life. The poor man of the South never is and cannot be made to be an independent and potential political or organic factor. He thinks and acts as he is advised and directed by his landlord, or the wealthy neighbor in whose clientage he belongs. The white " cropper " is almost as dependent for support upon his landlord as the colored tenant, and is far more easily controlled by threats or bribes, because he has no constant and abiding fear of the result of his action. To attribute to this class—the Southern poor whites—independent and harmonious action, according to a common method and design, throughout the Southern States, without the knowledge, approval and co-operation of the planters, lawyers, merchants and clergymen of the South, is as absurd as to suppose these acts to be perpetrated by children of tender years.

A suggestive view of this is given in the testimony of CORNELIUS McBRIDE, a school-teacher, who was whipped and driven out of Chickasaw Co., Miss., as follows:—

" Q. What is the character of the men who belong to this Ku-Klux organization?

" A. As a general thing they are an ignorant and illiterate set of men, and they seem to be determined to keep everybody else the same. The men who are engaged in Ku-Kluxing, if they were not sympathized with by men of better standing than themselves, would soon go under. This is easily shown. In the matter of bail, or anything of that kind, the best men of the community will give their signatures. In Oxford, for instance, when those men [who had whipped him and others] were arrested and brought there, they were put in pretty good quarters among the soldiers. But the people of the county had a meeting for their benefit, and took them beds, and chairs, and playing-cards, and all that. We believe that about one-half the white people in our county belong to the organization, from the fact that if you denounce the Ku-Klux, or take any action against them, you make one-half the people there your

THE BETTER CLASS OF POOR WHITES.

enemies, and they show it by condemning you. The president of the Board of Supervisors in my county asked me what kind of evidence I had against these fellows; I told him I had several colored witnesses and some white witnesses. He said, ' You must not bring colored testimony against white men in this county.' " (Vol. 11: p. 339.)

The above is the *most favorable* view of it possible to be taken—namely, that the perpetrators of the outrages were of the lower classes, aided and directed by their betters. Other victims—Northern men capable of judging—affirm that the bands of operators themselves contained intelligent, well-dressed, educated men. The truth probably lies between the two views, and varied with the locality.

Concerning the following points there is considerable conflict of testimony, viz. :

1.—As to the purpose and object for which the Klan was organized, and the motive and *rationale* of the various acts of outrage and violence shown to have been perpetrated by its members.

2.—As to the sentiment of the masses of the whites in regard to the blacks.

3.—As to the sentiment of the majority of the Southern whites in regard to native and non-native Republicans, or those who differed from the members of the Klan in regard to the status and rights of the negro.

These points are noted here merely to attract attention to those portions of the testimony of different witnesses and numerous unquestionable facts which will hereafter be laid before the reader. The purpose of this work being to enable the reader to form his own conclusions, only such hints will be given from time to time as may aid in reaching a proper conception of the subject in hand.

## CHAPTER V.

### DECLARED MOTIVES OF ACTION.

THERE can hardly be any fairer way of determining the motives of this organization than to take the statements of its own members. These may be divided into two classes : 1, the reasons given for the outrages to their victims, or to other parties concerning them, and 2, the "notices" or "warnings" served upon obnoxious individuals in the form of threats.

The case of ABRAM COLBY (Georgia) furnishes a fair sample of the reason alleged in at least two-thirds of the cases where a reason was assigned by the parties committing the outrage. He testifies:

"After they had whipped me a long time, they said I had voted for Grant, Bullock, and Blodgett. . . . They asked, 'Do you think you will ever vote another damned Radical ticket?' I said, 'I will not tell a lie.' They said, 'No, don't tell any lie.' Then I said, 'If there was an election to-morrow I would vote the Radical ticket.' I thought they would kill me anyhow. Then they set in to whipping me again." (Vol. 7: p. 696.)

17

Frequently, the motive announced was that of self-protection (not against violence, but against legal punishment for having committed violence). Mr. Cason, a Deputy United States Marshal, was killed in White County, Georgia, in 1867. Soon after, a large number of colored people living in the immediate vicinity of the killing were whipped and cruelly maltreated. H. D. INGERSOLL testifies:—

"Several negroes were whipped because it was supposed that they gave information as to who had killed Deputy Marshall Cason." (Vol. 7: p. 1172.)

18

Several instances of this will appear in the condensed experiences given farther on. This was the only cause assigned for the hanging of Wyatt Outlaw in Alamance County, N. C.,

and, it may be remembered, is the motion assigned in Part I.
for the hanging of "Uncle Jerry."

Again, it was frequently the case that a man was whipped
or killed for threatening or resisting the Klan. A case related
by Hon. A. WRIGHT, of Georgia, an ex-judge and ex-Congressman, illustrates this:—

"This negro had done nothing wrong. He had just talked
large about the Ku-Klux—the fight he would make if they
came for him. He had never been attacked, but some of his
race in that vicinity had. These young men went there and got
him to go with them to ku-klux the Ku-Klux, and having got
him out, shot or stabbed him [to death], I forget which. So
this young man, my client, who was one of them, told me."
(Vol. 6: p. 107.)

The excuse of a necessary police force is best stated in the
testimony of WILLIAM M. LOWE, born and raised and still living in Huntsville, Ala., lawyer, prosecuting attorney, &c. :—

"The justification or excuse which was given for the organization of the Ku-Klux Klan was that it was essential to preserve society; they thought after such a civil convulsion as we
had had in this country, the feebleness with which the laws
were executed, the disturbed state of society, it was necessary
that there should be some patrol of some sort, especially for
the country districts outside of town; that it had been a legal
and recognized mode of preserving the peace and keeping order
in the former condition of these States." (Vol. 9: p. 877.)

The reader who is desirous of knowing something more
about the old "patrol" and its character will find it considered at some length in a succeeding chapter.

Hon. DAVID SCHENCK, now a Judge of the Superior Court
of North Carolina, then a practising lawyer and member of the
Invisible Empire, and a Democrat, in his testimony before the
committee very forcibly states the view of one who had experience:—

"I was assured that it was merely a secret political society
to promote the interests of the Democratic party. . . . I
think it originated as a political society. . . . I think that
the society was political in its origin. . . . Its object was
to oppose and reject the principles of the Radical party."

The constitution of the Klan appended to Mr. Schenck's testimony shows how this purpose was to be effected. It purports to be the constitution of a Klan in South Carolina, but Judge Schenck testifies that he thought the organization that he joined was an offshoot of the organization in South Carolina.

"CONSTITUTION.

"ARTICLE I. This organization shall be known as the ——— Order, No.———, of the Ku-Klux Klan of the State of South Carolina.

"ARTICLE II. The officers shall consist of a Cyclops and a Scribe, both of whom shall be elected by a majority of the order, and to hold their office during good behavior.

"ARTICLE III., SECTION I. It shall be the duty of the C. to preside in the order, enforce a due observance of the constitution and by-laws, and exact compliance with the rules and usages of the order; to see that all the members perform their respective duties; appoint all committees before the order; *inspect the arms and dress of each member on special occasions;* to call meetings when necessary; draw upon members for all sums needed to carry on the order.

"SECTION II. The S. shall keep a record of the proceedings of the order; write communications; *notify other Klans when assistance is needed;* give notice when any member has to *suffer the penalty for violating his oath;*" &c., &c.

ARTICLE IV. provides that "no person of color shall be admitted to this order;" nor any one who is "in any way incapacitated *to perform the duties of a Ku-Klux.*"

"The C. shall have power to appoint such members to attend to . . . those *suffering from radical misrule,* as the case may require." (Art. I., Sec. 3.)

When a member is charged with violating his oath, a committee of five shall be appointed to investigate the matter, and Sec. 6 of Art. VI. provides that "when the committee report that the charges are sustained, and the unanimous vote of the members is given thereon, the offending person shall be sentenced to death by the Chief." Section 7, provides for a pardon:—"The person, through the Cyclops of the order of which he is a member, can make application to the Great Grand Cyclops of *Nashville, Tennessee,* in which case execution of the sentence can be stayed until pardoning power is heard from."

Perhaps this accounts for some of General Forrest's "one

hundred to one hundred and fifty letters a day from all over the South" !

↘ The means by which a member was to perform "the duties of a Ku-Klux" are given in Art. V., Sec. 1:—"Each member shall provide himself with a pistol, Ku-Klux gown and signal instrument." The fact that Judge Schenck did not look upon this as a mere unmeaning parade is shown by the fact that after declaring that he had left the order, he says :—"There are many ways of getting out of a difficulty ; one is to fight out and one is to back out. I backed out." In explanation of the backing-out process, he says it consisted simply in not going to any more meetings, though he afterwards talked with members in regard to its affairs. Being asked if he had denounced the Klan and openly and publicly severed his connection with it, he replied, "I did not dare to do so." And being asked what he feared, he answered, "I think if I had publicly denounced them I would have incurred their displeasure. I feared personal violence. . . . I would not have done it for any amount of money. . . . I say candidly, I should have been endangering my life to have done so."

Judge Schenck was an original secessionist, a member of the Secession Convention of North Carolina in 1861, and a valiant fire-eater until war began. After three months' service as a Confederate Commissary, he tired of war's alarms and became a Confederate tax-collector or tithing-master for the counties of Lincoln and Gaston while the war lasted. He is of an excellent family and of the best social and political standing until this day. His testimony may be found in Vol. 2, *K. K. Rep.*, pp. 362 to 415.

In order to trace the connection between General Forrest's "Invisible Empire" and such inferior "realms" or "dominions" of it as the above document would go to indicate, as well as to suggest the high and holy aims of the order, we may here look at a few of the provisions of the *Prescript* or *Constitution* referred to in Chap. III.

21

### " CREED.

" We, the * * reverently acknowledge the Majesty and Supremacy of the Divine Being, and recognize the goodness and providence of the same.

"PREAMBLE.

"We recognize our relations to the United States Government, and acknowledge the supremacy of its laws.

"APPELLATION.

"ARTICLE I. This organization shall be styled and denominated the * * .

"TITLES.

"ARTICLE II. The officers of this * shall consist of a Grand Wizard of the Empire and his ten Genii ; a Grand Dragon of the Realm and his eight Hydras ; a Grand Titan of the Dominion and his six Furies ; a Grand Giant of the Province and his four Goblins ; a Grand Cyclops of the Den and his two Night-Hawks ; a Grand Magi, a Grand Monk, a Grand Exchequer, a Grand Turk, a Grand Scribe, a Grand Sentinel, and a Grand Ensign.

"SEC. 2. The body-politic of this * shall be designated and known as Ghouls." [ !]

Then follow various articles, edicts, &c., closing with this affecting

"L'ENVOI.

"To the lovers of law and order, peace and justice, we send you greeting ; and to the shades of the venerated dead we affectionately dedicate the † † ."

[Whether "††" means "the daggers," or something more recondite, must be left to the reader's ingenuity.]

The other source of information as to the spirit and animus which led this secret army to assail their unarmed and helpless victims in every State of the South with such unanimity of action is the language of the notices and warnings served on intended victims and persons obnoxious to its membership. And inasmuch as these are the declarations made by the Ku-Klux themselves, it must commend itself to all as a peculiarly fair and reliable method of obtaining such information.

These notices, served on men by being left at their doors or sent to them in some secret way, were of almost every conceivable form—coffins, knives, and written or printed letters, adorned with symbolic figures. The skull and cross-bones were favorite devices. There were very few prominent Union men or Republicans who did not receive more or less numerous warnings of this character. Many testify that they had received several. They were usually followed by some demonstration against the party threatened, but not always. Sometimes several "camps" or "dens" would, independently of each other, direct a warning to be sent to the same individual. The writer has seen hundreds of these, and has received a number of them himself. They are valuable not only as showing the real animus of the writers, but also as disclosing the sentiments of a community in which these things were almost as common as anything in nature. We give some few samples, preceding them with the names of the recipients :—

ALFRED RICHARDSON, a prosperous and thrifty colored man, of Clarke County, Georgia, testifies to having received the following :—

"They say you are making too much money [he was keeping a grocery], and they do not allow any nigger to rise that way; that you can control all the colored votes, and they intend to break you up and run you off so that they can control the balance." (Vol. 6: pp. 1–6.) 22

Of the same character are the following, to three of the tenants of Jerry Owens, a colored man of industry and thrift, of Tatnall County, Georgia, who had been previously run off by them, but still held his lands.

"HENRY FRAZER: We see that you are building on Jerry Owens' place. You must stop at once and vacate in 30 days. When you leave set fire to all the buildings, as it will save us the trouble of doing it. Do it in 30 days; if you don't, when we come we will treat you harshly. So get out in 30 days or you will have to suffer the consequences."
"Tatnall Co., Dec. 15th, 1870.

"ADAM STAFFORD: The object of this note is to inform you that you must vacate Jerry Owens' place. He was run off and his house burnt, and now you are building and improving it. You have been informed once not to do it. Now, for the last time, you must vacate that place in one month, or you will be visited and dealt with harshly. When you leave set fire to all the houses and fences. We will come to see you in 30 days if you don't leave."
"Tatnall Co., Dec. 13th, 1870. 23

"To THOMAS ALLEN (freedman) : You are in great danger; you are going heedless with the Radicals and against the white population. . . . Just vote or use your influence for the Radicals, and you go up, certain. . . . You are marked and watched closely by the K. K. K."

"By order of the GRAND CYCLOPS." (Vol. 7: p. 610.)

These notices were not obeyed, and a terrible punishment 24 followed.

JOHN TAYLOR COLEMAN (white) ; President of Demopolis, Marengo Co., Alabama; Mail Route Agent on North and South Alabama R. R. ; appointed by influence of Representative Hays (Rep.) ; left the road because he was threatened by the K. K., who had shortly before shot a colored mail route agent in broad daylight, in his postal car, on this road. Reason : they did not intend to allow any negro route agents, or negro firemen, or negro brakesmen, on the road. The notice to Coleman was a letter which he got from the Calera post-office, a copy of which may be seen on the page opposite.

This man was too wise to disregard the warning given, and 25 so no doubt saved his life.

The following batch of notices present some interesting features. They were presented by the witness whose testimony is given in brief with them :—

26     JOS. H. SPEED: Born and educated in Virginia, lived for some time in North Carolina, and then removed to Alabama. Has lived in Marion, Perry County, since 1858. Never been out of the South till after the war. Was a school-teacher when war broke out; an officer in Confederate army from near beginning of the war till appointed by Governor of Alabama as State Agent at the Virginia Salt Works. After war was member of Alabama Constitutional Convention, and joined Republican party when the Republican Legislature removed all disfranchisements in the State. Married twice, ladies of Perry County families. Is now Register and Master of Chancery Court of his District.

Testifies that an Englishman named Geo. A. Clark was teaching negro school in Sumter County; band of men took him out,

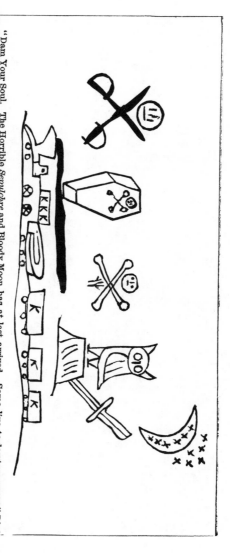

"Dam Your Soul. The Horrible *Sepulchre* and Bloody Moon has at last arrived. Some live to-day to-morrow "*Die*," We the undersigned understand through our Grand "*Cyclops*" that you have recommended a big Black Nigger for Male agent on our nu rode; wel, sir, Jest you understand in time if he gets on the rode you can make up your mind to pull roape. If you have anything to say in regard to the Matter, meet the Grand Cyclops and Conclave at Den No. 4 at 12 o clock mid-night, Oct. 1st, 1871. When you were in Calera we warned you to hold your tounge and not speak so much with your mouth or otherwise You will be taken on surprise and led out by the Klan and learnt to stretch hemp. Beware. Beware. Beware. Beware.

(Signed)

"PHILLIP ISENBAUM.
" JOHN BANKSTOWN.
" ESAU DAVES, *Grand Cyclops.*
" MARCUS THOMAS.
" BLOODY BONES.

"You know who. And all others of the Klan."

SPECIMEN OF A KU-KLUX NOTICE.

whipped him very severely, shot him and hung him, leaving him for dead. He crawled off and recovered.

Testifies: "When I was in Tuscaloosa to take part in reorganizing the university, Professor Whitfield, a Professor in the institution, gave me some letters which I have here, which were addressed to students of the university. There were only a very few students there. These letters had a string tied around them, and were hung upon this dagger [witness produces a dagger], which was stuck into one of the doors of the university. One of these students was the son of ex-Governor Smith. The letters are as follows:—

"DAVID SMITH : You have received one notice from us, and this shall be our last. You nor no other d——d son of a d——d radical traitor shall stay at our university. Leave here in less than ten days, for in that time we will visit the place and it will not be well for you to be found out there. The State is ours, and so shall our university be. Written by the secretary by order of the Klan."

"SEAVEY : You have received one notice from us to leave. This is the last. We will be out in force in less than ten days, and it will not be good for you to be found out there. We are resolved it shall not be carried on under the present faculty. Some have been wise enough to take our warning. Do the same. The Klan."

"CHARLES MUNCEL : You had better get back where you came from. We don't want any d——d Yank at our colleges. In less than ten days we will come to see if you obey our warning. If not look out for hell, for, d—n you, we will show you that you shall not stay, you nor no one else in that college. This is your first notice; let it be your last. The Klan, by the Secretary."

"HORTON : They say you are of good democratic family. If you are, leave the university, and that quick. We don't intend that the concern shall run any longer. This is the second notice that you have received; you will get no other. In less than ten days we intend to clean out the concern. We *will* have good southern men there or none. By order of the K. K. K."

"This Charles Muncel, to whom one of the letters was addressed, was a young man from the State of New York, as I was informed by one of the faculty.

"Q. Did those students leave ?

"A. They left; they were smart enough for that." (Vol. 8: p. 419.)

With these sample declarations of the intent of the redoubtable Klan to labor for the political and social regeneration of the South in their own peculiar fashion, we may pass on to other points, repeating, however, what has been said above, that these, and the other indications to be found hereafter, while varying in immediate application, all point to the same principle, namely: that negroes and Northerners who presume to differ from their neighbors in politics are not to be tolerated at the South on a plane of political equality with the native whites.

Fair-minded Northerners will hope that this is an exaggeration; fair-minded Southerners will see in it nothing strange, and will only wonder why so much pother is made about a matter of course.

## CHAPTER VI.

### THE DISGUISES AND MODES OF OPERATION.

The character of the disguises worn, their completeness and uniformity of style, shed no little light upon the character and purposes of the organization. The cut which is given at page 225 of Part I. is drawn directly from a disguise captured on a North Carolina Ku-Klux who was an officer of the Klan. The following descriptions will show how it corresponded with the disguises worn by them in Georgia, Alabama and Mississippi. It will be remarked that in its early stages the uniform seems to have been generally white, perhaps to correspond with one of the names adopted, "The White Brotherhood." Afterwards it seems to have been universally black with red trimmings.

Mr. G. B. Burnett, in describing a raid which was made upon him in Summerville, Georgia, in 1870, when he was a Republican candidate for Congress, says:—

"About 12 o'clock I heard whistles about over the town, and knew in a moment what it was. . . . . They were dressed in what appeared to be white gowns, and their horses were also disguised. I could not tell exactly what their disguises were, though I looked as close as I could. I took it to be a white gown over their persons and a white sheet over their horses." (Vol. 7: p. 849.)

Though he says he knew everybody in the county, he failed to recognize one of them.

Mr. C. C. Hughes gives the following description of the Georgia Ku-Klux:—

"They had something over their bodies similar to gowns. I have a cap here which was found at the place where I was whipped, next morning. There was a stick placed in the hind part of this cap to make it stand up straight. And there are holes here, as you can see, for the eyes and mouth and nose, marked by some red stuff." (Vol. 6: p. 540.)

Rev. A. S. Lakin, the Methodist clergyman already quoted,

who because of his connection with the Northern branch of that church seems to have been an object of especial aversion to the Klan, thus describes their uniform in Alabama:—

"I have myself seen the Klan riding on several occasions. They were very hideous. They generally wear very high caps, of a conical form, very tall and running up to a point, and without brim; with eye and mouth holes, heavy mustaches and long beards painted, generally with long black gowns. Their signals are given by means of whistles, common hunting whistles, similar to those you will hear for starting street cars." (Vol 8 : p. 120.)

JOHN A. MINNIS, born and raised in North Carolina; lived in Tennessee from 1838 to 1866, and since then in Alabama; lawyer, now (1871) U. S. Dist. Attorney for N. Dist. Alabama, describing the disguise of parties on a raid into Eutaw, Ala., says:—

"They were disguised with black loose gowns, with something that covered their faces, something like quills that made them look like long, big teeth, and made a peculiar sort of noise. They were on horseback, the horses being disguised by having black hung over them." (Vol. 8 : p. 528–9.)

WILLIAM H. LENTZ, native of Limestone Co., Ala.; always lived there; Sheriff of the county; says:—

"I have seen portions of the Ku-Klux in their costumes, three times, I think. They were mounted, their horses covered—disguised. I have seen of late (1870–1) some disguises that were captured the other day, and they compare very well with those worn in 1868. The disguise covered the body, the head and the face. There is long hair, I suppose about a foot long, coming out of the face, as if it were mustaches, hanging down at least a foot. I do not know where they were manufactured, but they showed some skill in the construction." (Vol. 9 : p. 723.)

The following is the testimony of one who might well rank as an expert on the subject:—

JAMES M. MOSS, farmer. Lived near Huntsville, Ala., since 1866 (five years). Has seen disguised bands six different times, varying from 3 to 30, all mounted, armed, horses and men disguised.

"Nobody can tell who they are, for some of them have a

sort of a mouth-piece with them to talk through that don't make a natural tone at all, and then their faces are covered up. What I call our home-made Ku-Klux have rather a cheap rig on by the side of our ordinary Ku-Klux. This gown I found was just a loose gown with big long sleeves to it, and then they have a piece of the long gown thrown up over the head if they want it, but it has eye-holes, and all Christendom could not tell who was inside of it by seeing the eyes. What I call the Tennessee Ku-Klux had a very good rig. They look pretty well, with a red coat trimmed off with black, and when they threw the piece up over, it was lined with different color from the rest. They had a sort of rubber cape with fixings to come all over them in a rain-storm. They could wear that down." (Vol. 9 : p. 919.)

Geo. Taylor (colored) Methodist Episcopal preacher, married, industrious, who was severely whipped and driven away from Stevenson, Ala., describes his assailants thus:—

"There were twelve of them. They had on something like an old-fashioned hunting-shirt, as they have them in this southern part. They had a belt around them, and were buttoned plumb up here, and had a black gown that came all around; some had black gowns and some other colors. They were of different colors. Over their heads they had what seemed to me like a cloth; it had marks made over it for eye-brows, and holes cut for eyes, and a place for the nose, and they were tied around the neck and back of the head below in some way under the chin. Some of them had something like horns." (Vol. 8 : p. 574.)

Joseph Gill (colored) was whipped by the Ku-Klux (200 lashes) and shot at twice because he refused to give up his horse, which they said they wanted to ride back to hell. They said they came from there, and had couriers from there nine times a day, and they wanted that horse to "tote" them. They visited him again, searching for arms:—

"They had on gowns just like your overcoat, that came down to the toes; and some would be red and some black, like a lady's dress, only open before. The hats were made of paper, and about eighteen inches long, and at the top about as thick as your ankle, and down around the eyes it was bound like horse-covers, and on the mouth there was hair of some description, I don't know what. It looked like a mustache, coming down to the breast, and you couldn't see none of the face, nor nothing. You couldn't see a thing of them. Some had horns about as long as my finger, and made black. They said they came from hell; that they died at Shiloh fight and Bull Run." (Vol. 9 : pp. 813, 814.)

The uniform of the Mississippi Ku-Klux may be gathered from the following interesting description given by Col. A. P. HUGGINS of the disguise worn by the K. K. band of 120 men who whipped him near Aberdeen, Monroe Co., Miss., on the night of March 9, 1870 (Vol. 11 : pp. 273, 274):—

"The gown they had on came just about half-way down below the knee; it was cut rather like a tight night-gown, and was close fitting over their coats, and slashed up on each side, so as to allow them to step well. There was a band around the waist, and all up and down, in front of their gowns, were the same sort of buttons; that struck me as another singular thing; they were all pearl buttons. Their head-piece, the front of it, was a piece of cloth rounded to a point, and came down to about the pit of the stomach, long enough to cover the beards of most of them; but I saw the beards of some of them even under that—those who had long beards. In these face-pieces were large round holes for the eyes, two inches across. The hole for the mouth in the face-piece was a very large hole. Around these mouth-holes and eye-holes were rings of red, to make them look like blood; I do not know what they were stained with. The back part of the head-piece, when placed around in front, came down just over the eye-brows; when riding, or not at their work, they always put their head-pieces on with the long piece back, and the back piece in front, in order to give them an unobstructed view. They could turn it around, and let the long round piece hang down behind when they were riding; many times they have been seen in that way in the country. The color was pure white; there was no difference in color. . . . Their clothing was all of the same pattern and form; they were all cut and made garments."

The portability of this disguise is a matter of importance. The utmost ingenuity was displayed in its construction to effect this end. The one from which the illustration is taken could easily be folded and pushed in one side of the ordinary saddle-bags in use in that country. By this means men could ride along the roads in open day or at night on their way to the appointed rendezvous in their ordinary garb and attract no attention. It was for this reason, too, that a single masked and disguised Ku-Klux was hardly ever met upon the roads. The disguise was assumed at the place of assembly, and removed immediately after their work was done, and they dispersed in peace to their homes.

The method of procedure among the Klans does not fully appear from the volumes of the Report, since at that time very few of the members had made confession, and the few who were willing to disclose its workings feared to do so because of its power. In the winter and spring of 1873, however, numerous members of the Klan, becoming apprehensive of punishment, made confession and revealed the secret working of the Klan. From several hundred of these confessions which have been put at our disposal we select some passages which may throw light on the methods of the Klan. Owing to the fact that all the perpetrators of these crimes have been amnestied by special act, and that it might be unpleasant if not unsafe for the parties who made confession, their names will be suppressed. The confessions, however, are all legal documents, duly signed and sworn to before a subscribing officer of Court.

27

Says one:—

"I was a member of Camp No. 3, and I was sent to meet a party from Camp No. 7, and guide them to the residence of ————— and —————. I do not know what camp passed the order that these parties should be visited. I only did as I was directed."

Another says:—

"It was the usual thing for one camp to pass sentence and another to execute it. Whenever an order was received from another camp the Chief was required to detail men to perform it, no matter what it might be."

One who had been sent to pilot a party from another camp said:—

"I met J. B —— with a detail of men from his camp, and there was a squad from ours, but we had no Chief there. I do not know what camp passed the decree, nor do I know what it was. When I was ordered to go and act as pilot, I was told that certain men were to be visited. I don't remember that I was told what was to be done with them. When we met, nobody seemed to know what it was. A squad was to have come from the Sheriff's camp with the orders, but they did not get there in time. So it was put to a vote whether he should be whipped or hanged. A majority voted in favor of hanging. We voted with the uplifted hand."

Another, who was a poor man, said :—

"I was initiated in Mr. ——'s store, and went on two raids. I had no horse, but rode J. E.'s on those occasions. Then I got scared and did not go near the camp again for some weeks. I met the Chief one day, who said to me that if I didn't do better I'd get "visited" myself. I told him I couldn't go on raids because I had no horse. He said there needn't be any trouble on that account. There were *plenty of men who couldn't go on raids who had good horses* that I could get. I went on a good many raids after that, and *always had a horse furnished me.*"

Another said :—

"I was ordered to meet a party who were coming from Stokes County, at a certain cross-roads. I understood that the orders were to interrupt Judge Settle on his way home from Raleigh, and tie him on the bridge nigh his house and burn it up. There had been a heap of trouble about that bridge, and the Camp allowed they'd get rid of the bridge and the Judge at once. I didn't go because I was sick, but I heard afterwards that the Judge didn't come." *

These perhaps sufficiently illustrate the main feature of their operations.

Very great surprise has been felt at the North that such an organization could carry on such wholesale outrage with so slight a percentage of accident or fatality occurring to themselves. The inquiry is always made, "Why did the victims not fight?" Fight whom? Fight when? When attacked, it was a hundred against one, in the dead of night, with the added chances of almost invariable surprise. And as for punishing the malefactors afterwards, whom would you select? "I did not know one of them from Adam," was the universal statement. But added to this was the fact that almost universally the first thing done was to disarm the negroes and leave

* See "A Fool's Errand," pp. 262-3.

them defenceless. From all parts of the country came testimony like this of WILLIAM FORD (colored), Huntsville, Ala:—

"Have frequently heard of Ku-Klux visiting the colored people's houses for the purpose of taking their arms of defense. They called on me for my arms that night. I had none. They took the arms from mighty near all the colored people in the neighborhood. In 1868, men that claimed to be Ku-Klux, from each way, so far as I could learn, went about the country taking arms away from the colored men in all parts of the country." (Vol. 9: p. 683.)

Or that of GEORGE CORNELIUS (Vol. 9: p. 1195), who says:—

"There is not a colored man in all my country who has or dared have a gun or pistol. The Ku-Klux took them all and threatened to kill any one who should keep one."

28

Or that of a colored soldier who was beaten for having served the country and fought for his own liberty—GEORGE ROPER (colored), Huntsville:—

"The Ku-Klux took a great many arms from the people that year; pistols, and guns, and I don't know what. This man says to me, 'You were a colored soldier; you was a man that fought against your master.' I said, 'Yes, Sir, I was in the Union Army and fought for my liberty. I was called and I went.'" (Vol 9: p. 689.)

JOHN H. NAGER, Disbursing Agent Freedman's Bureau, gives a list of 61 names, colored men, who were visited by men in disguise, threatened, whipped, and deprived of their guns, between the fall of 1868 and 1871. Also notes several cases of hanging, and threats of death and whipping if they should vote at election, or if they did not vote the Democratic ticket. This all in Madison Co., Ala. (Vol. 9: pp. 928–931.)

It should be remembered that the several legislatures first convened after the war enacted what were termed " Black Codes," which forbade colored people " to keep firearms of any kind," and made the possession of such a criminal offense which was punishable by a fine equal to twice the value of the weapon so unlawfully kept, or, "if that be not immediately paid, by corporeal punishment." These Black Codes farther exemplified the spirit of the Klan and show to what feeling it owes its origin by providing that "no person of color shall

29

pursue or practice the art, trade, or business of an artisan, mechanic or shopkeeper, or any other trade or employment (beside that of husbandry or that of a servant under contract for labor), until he shall have obtained a license, which license shall be good only for *one year.*" The fee for such license ran from $10 to $100 per annum, and no such license was exacted from the whites. The evident purpose of it all was to handicap the negro with unequal conditions so as to prevent the possibility of his rise in the scale of wealth and intelligence.

The vagrant laws, which constituted a part of these "Black Codes," were models of cunning and deliberate cruelty. Men and women were compelled to let their labor by contract, and those who failed to do so within a certain period were seized as "vagrants," their labor sold by the sheriff at public outcry to the highest bidder to pay the costs and fine. Colored people traveling in other counties or districts than those in which they resided without a certificate or pass from the "Master" or "Mistress" who employed them, were liable to be seized and sold in like manner. Such a vagrant law, in its main features, is now in force in the State of Alabama. In some instances employers have combined together, agreeing not to pay more than two dollars per month for such "vagrant" labor. As the fine and costs usually range from $30 to $50, it will be seen that such a law establishes a very reasonable substitute for the Slavery which preceded it.

The "Black Code" of Louisiana was perhaps the most infamous piece of legislative brutality that ever disgraced the statute-book of a Christian land : "In that State all agricultural laborers were compelled to make labor contracts during the first ten days of January, for the next year. The contract once made, the laborer was not to be allowed to leave his place of employment during the year except upon conditions not likely to happen and easily prevented. The master was allowed to make deductions of the servants' wages for 'injuries done to animals and agricultural implements committed to his care,' thus making the negroes responsible for wear and tear. Deductions were to be made for 'bad or negligent work,' the

master being the judge. For every act of 'disobedience' a
fine of one dollar was imposed on the offender—disobedience
being a technical term made to include, besides 'neglect of
duty,' and 'leaving home without permission,' such fearful
offenses as 'impudence,' or 'swearing,' or 'indecent language in the presence of the employer, his family, or agent,'
or 'quarreling or fighting with one another.' The master or
his agent might assail every ear with profaneness aimed at the
negro men, and outrage every sentiment of decency in the foul
language addressed to the negro women ; but if one of the
helpless creatures, goaded to resistance and crazed under
tyranny, should answer back with impudence, or should relieve
his mind with an oath, or retort indecency upon indecency, he
did so at the cost to himself of one dollar for every outburst.
The 'agent' referred to in the statute is the well-known overseer of the cotton region, and the care with which the law-
makers of Louisiana provided that his delicate ears and sensi-
tive nerves should not be offended with an oath or an indecent word from a negro will be appreciated by all who have
heard the crack of the whip on a Southern plantation."

The spirit of these codes was but continued and carried into
operation by the various unlawful operations which afterward
sprung up and *still* hold sway in that section. The cruelty
which we find upon the statute-book is the same spirit which
was exemplified upon the midnight raid—nothing more and
nothing less: the one was the legitimate fruit and offspring of
the other. The former was shielded by the mocking sanction of
public law; the latter by the impenetrable disguise of the Klan.
The heart which conceived the one guided the hand which performed the other. Both were the natural fruit of the institution of Slavery, the outcome and incidents of a "chivalry"
which was fair and white without, but "full of dead men's
bones within."

In connection with this it should be remembered that
the colored people are the most peaceably disposed race
upon earth. They are willing to submit to almost any
affront in order to avoid trouble or strife. They have always

been in a servile position and accustomed to the domination and arrogance of the white race. To such an extent was this carried even in the most conservative of the Southern States, North Carolina, that the common law was warped and twisted to suit the feeling and prejudices of the times, by its supreme judicial tribunal, until it came to be the law of the land that impudent or disrespectful words from a free colored man justified an assault upon him by a white man, and resistance to such an assault justified a killing. They were accustomed to having their houses entered by the patrol before the war, and instinctively obeyed whenever a white man commanded. They were all "croppers" or "hirelings" too, after the war, and the general impression, in some cases the express law, is that the owner has the right to enter the dwellings assigned to each without their consent. The first care of the Ku-Klux was to disarm their victims, and every one who resisted met a terrible fate. (See the story of the Jeffers family, given elsewhere.)

No better instance of this peaceful, forbearing, and long-suffering spirit of the colored race can be given ,than the fact that although they well knew that the outcome of the war of rebellion was to decide upon the continuation or termination of the state of bondage in which they were then held, and, though all the able-bodied white men were in the Confederate Army, they were guilty of no outrages upon the defenceless women and children left in their care, but wrought peaceably and quietly for their support during the entire war, and were tenderly respectful of them afterwards. Of this fact there can be no better or more competent witness that General J. B. GORDON, who commanded Stonewall Jackson's corps after his death, and is now United States Senator from Georgia. He says:—

"As a general thing, the negroes have behaved so well since the war that it is a common remark in Georgia that no race on earth, released from servitude under the circumstances they were, would have behaved so well. I have said so in public speeches. The behaviour of the negroes during the war was remarkable. When almost the entire white male population old enough to bear arms was in the army, and large plantations were left to be managed by women and children, not a single

THE OBSTREPEROUS AFRICAN.

insurrection had occurred, not a life had been taken; and that, too, when the Federal armies were marching through the country with freedom, as was understood, upon their banners. Scarcely an outrage occurred. The negroes generally understood that if the South should be whipped their freedom would be the result. I notified my slaves of it early in the war, I think it was in 1863." (Vol. 6: p. 334.)   30

Yet General Gordon testifies (p. 308) that a sort of "brotherhood" was established in Georgia, in 1865–6, for self-protection against these well-behaving people, because the Union League and the carpet-baggers were organizing them, and the white natives feared them. He denies that their organization had disguises; and that may easily have been so at the commencement; yet the history of the doings of the Ku-Klux in Georgia, in 1868–70, differs in nothing from the murderous record of the disguised midnight "ghouls" in the other States. And, while on General Gordon's testimony, we may note a single question and answer concerning the "carpet-bag government" of Georgia, as late as 1870:—

"*Question.*—Governor Bullock states in a recent publication, that of all the State officers, elected by the people or appointed by himself, there are not more than a dozen men holding offices (and those offices unimportant) who are not either natives of the State or residents of the State before the war.

"*Answer.*—I presume that is true."   31

## CHAPTER VII.

### WHO WERE THE VICTIMS.

As has already been stated, it appears that in almost every instance the victims were negro Republicans. The few cases in which they were of no politics at all or of the contrary mode of thought seem to have been either those who had given some offence to the order generally, or against whom individuals of the Klan had some special grudge. There can be no doubt that the Klan was not unfrequently made the instrument of private malice and revenge, and in not a few cases of individual greed.

There is a class of cases, too, of which the reader will find several instances in these pages, where the motive seems to have been a general envy or animosity towards negroes who were getting along too fast in the world, in the opinion of their white neighbors.

Upon this point of the character of the victims the exceptions made to the general rule by ex-Judge and ex-Congressman Hon. A. R. WRIGHT, of Georgia, is very suggestive. After having mentioned and sought to excuse various outrages, he is asked:—

"Q. Have you ever known an instance in which the Ku-Klux committed an outrage upon a member of the Democratic party?

"A. I know one instance. They whipped a man *for ku-kluxing without leave from the head man.* . . . They also whipped a white man *who helped a negro in a fight.* I think he voted the Democratic ticket. It has generally been negroes and radicals they were after." (Vol. 6: pp. 114–115.)

32

Illustrative of another class is the following:

"If they have any difficulty with a negro he is reported to the Ku-Klux. I noticed that just about the time they (the negroes) got done laying by their crops, the Ku-Klux would be brought in and they would be run off so that they (the owners of the land) could take their crops."

J. R. HOLLIDAY, Georgia.

(Vol. 6: p. 420.)

"Negroes and whites, but principally negroes, have been killed, whipped and imposed on in various ways. It has been very common for two years—so common that it would take a *right sharp case now to attract much attention!*"

G. B. BURNET, Georgia.

(Vol. 7: p. 949.)

The same witness (who was a candidate for Congress in 1870) testifies of a colored man named Jourdan Ware, who was beaten, and says:—

"The reason they gave for beating him was that he had made some insulting remarks to a white lady. He remarked, 'How d'ye, sis?' or something of that kind, as the young lady passed down the road. Previous to that time he had borne the reputation of being a humble and obedient negro. He had a little farm, and was doing well and was comfortable, *though in a neighborhood surrounded by the poorer class of white people, who did not like his residence there.* I do not say whether he did or did not make the remark, though from my knowledge of him my opinion is that he did not. . . . They shot a colored man named Joe Kennedy, and beat his wife, who was a bright colored woman. The charge they had against Joe Kennedy was that he had married this mulatto girl, and they did not intend that he should marry so white a woman as she was; and they beat her also for marrying so black a negro as he was" (pp. 74, 75).

But, after all, the generality of the cases, in all the States alike, will come under the explanations given in the testimony of Solicitor FORSYTH for the Rome Judicial district of Georgia (Vol. 7: pp. 25–27), from which we extract a few points. He had been testifying of some specific outrage that he knew of, and said that he had heard also of other similar crimes committed by these disguised bands in other parts of the State:—

"Q. Do you know the politics of the parties who were the victims of the outrages in your circuit?

"A. I think I do pretty generally.

"Q. Are the victims all of one party?

"A. I am not positive about this man Phant; all the others I know belong to the Republican party. . . .

" Q. Did the man [a captured Ku-Klux] intimate as to what was their purpose ?

" A. No, sir; nothing more than to keep the negroes in subordination.

" Q. You say there was nothing on the part of the negroes, in their conduct, that would warrant any such movement ?

" A. Nothing as a race.

" Q. They have been orderly and peaceable ?

" A. Except in individual instances.

" Q. Have you known a great many negroes to be taken from their houses and whipped ?  Have you heard it from reliable authority ?

" A. Yes, sir.

" Q. Any killed ?

" A. I have heard of their being killed.

" Q. You say you have had no difficulty in executing the law upon negroes when they have committed outrages ?

" A. No, sir; none at all.

" Q. Your difficulty has been in executing the law on these white men ?

" A. Yes, in identifying them.

" Q. Suppose you had the influence of the better part of the community earnestly given, would you not be able to ferret them out and identify them ?

" A. I think I would. . . .  There are men of considerable influence in the county who stand back and behind that sort of thing and encourage it.

" Q. What is the politics of those men ?

" A. Well, they run in the Democratic line.   The Republicans oppose it in a body and denounce it.

" Q. You think the cause of this thing was the emancipation of the slaves, as you said just now, and the conferring upon them civil rights, among other rights that of voting ?

" A. Yes, sir; that is my opinion.

" Q. The object of this organization is to prevent the free exercise by the negroes of such rights ?

" A. It is very hard for me to testify as to that being the object; I think it has that effect, but not being acquainted with the organization, I should dislike to testify that that is the object.

" Q. You think it is a general organization, and that it extends all over the State ?

" A. Yes, sir; my opinion is that it is intended to control the colored race in every respect, politically as well as in every other way, and to keep them in subjection to the whites.  And people justify it upon the ground that it is necessary to keep the negroes in subjection."

Perhaps nothing could be more instructive to the reader who desires to realize the condition of the public mind and the mental state of one to whom the victims came day after day, each with his tale of woe, than an extract from the testimony of CORNELIUS MCBRIDE, the white teacher of a colored school in Chickasaw County, Mississippi, already mentioned, who was himself brutally beaten, driven away from his work and compelled to flee the State. He gives a short account of the outrages which came to his ears in the few months previous to his own castigation, which is as follows:—

"Addy Foster was whipped in Winston County for buying land; I got this from William Coleman, his neighbor. William Miller told me he was whipped because they said he wouldn't raise his hat to a white man; this also in Winston County. Aleck Hughes, in Naxubee County, was whipped—a white man owed him $17, and he threatened to sue him for it, and they whipped him for doing so. Hughes gave me the statement himself. All those cases were by disguised men. They hung Aleck Hughes up by the neck and nearly killed him; he was insensible when they let him down. Zack Job was whipped in Naxubee County, and Henry Leadbetter was also whipped, both by disguised men, some time in March, 1871. In Corinth, Mississippi, George Shubble was whipped by disguised men, and near the same place Fanny Honeysuckle was whipped by disguised men; and John Campbell, who kept a grocery store, was whipped by this body of disguised men because he would not give them some whisky. A number of other men at Oxford told me of outrages upon them, but I omitted to note the counties. My information comes from the victims themselves or from Mr. Wiley, the U. S. District Attorney at Oxford." (Vol. 11: pp. 339, 340.)

Turning from their own declarations, we may take the opinions of a few of those who disclaim connection with it, that almost all who were maltreated, and nearly every Republican, white or black, who was examined, attribute to the organization a political motive.

LEWIS E. PEARSONS, lawyer, residing in Talladega, Ala., since 1839, testifies:—

"The State examined a witness, named Lewis M. Force,

who proved that he had been a member of the Ku-Klux Klan. He stated that the organization in Alabama numbered from eight to ten thousand members, and that it had from ten to twelve thousand members in Georgia, when he was initiated, with headquarters at Atlanta; that the object of the organization was to control the negro vote, and to defeat the Republican party in obtaining offices." (Vol. 8: p. 79.)

"From what I have seen and heard, I have formed the conclusion that the Ku-Klux organization was formed for the purpose of controlling the negro vote and the negro labor, to prevent the free exercise, on their part, of the rights which the Federal Government had conferred upon them. By controlling the negro's labor I mean that they intended he should work only for such persons and upon such terms as they sanctioned" (p. 92).

H. D. INGERSOLL, native of Gloucester, Mass., agent of mining company in Sandsville, Ga., since 1865:—

Thinks northern men and Republicans have no protection in the courts. Negroes were ordered to quit after crops were gathered, if they voted Republican ticket. States general feeling of those who call themselves the better classes, against northern men and all who do not conform to their ideas with regard to the negro, to be very bad. (Vol. 7: pp. 1171–1176.)

As to the violence used, Mr. Ingersoll very justly observes:—

"I do not think they generally want to do so much injury —sometimes they do. I think it is done, almost wholly, to intimidate men and control the country. They *do not generally use any harsher means than will accomplish their purpose.*" (Vol. 7: p. 1172.)

To be fair, it really does seem as though the Ku-Klux did not commit murders unless they had honestly made up their minds to do it, and in deliberative assembly "voted" to that end. Mere "outrages" were of less moment.

FRANCIS MARION HILL, native of Alabama, lived in Choctaw County ever since it was organized; by occupation a farmer, but has been magistrate, county treasurer, judge of probate and register in chancery.

After detailing how he was forced to resign his office of judge of probate (to which he had been appointed by the first Governor under Reconstructed State Government) by threats, anonymous K. K. K. letters, having his office shot into, and being himself shot in the arm on the roadside; and giving the circumstances of seven murders in the county at the hands of disguised bands:—he was asked if he had heard of any negroes being whipped in the county:—

"Well, I have heard of some, but I have paid so little attention to them—that was a matter of no importance—that I do not believe I could undertake to state anything of the sort. Unless a murder was committed it was not considered much at all." (Vol. 10: p. 1919.)

It will have been apparent, now, who were the victims of these operations; but nothing·like a just estimate of the number of murders and outrages committed by this organization ever has been or ever can be made. That thousands of lives were taken, and tens of thousands of acts of violence committed, there can be no doubt. That hundreds and perhaps thousands were beaten who never revealed the fact is the universal opinion of people resident in the infected regions, and very many cases which became known only by accident, or through the boastfulness or confession of some of the perpetrators, give ample color to this belief. The actual number, however, is unimportant from any point of view. The manner, character, and effect of the acts only are pertinent to any inquiry which may now be prosecuted—the manner and character as throwing light upon the motive and purpose of the organization, and the effect upon the public mind, or the minds of those who were likely to be victims, as a measure of the barbarity necessary to achieve the results intended.

When it is remembered that the perpetrators of all these crimes are unpunished, and that the crimes were committed by ever-present bands of disguised men, who may have been, in any case, composed of the victim's nearest neighbors, and perhaps his most open and pronounced sympathizers, some idea of the reign of terror produced among those classes who were subject to such attacks may be obtained. At the same time, it will be seen that those whose relations with the membership of the Klan were such as to preclude the probability of attack, might well testify that they felt no apprehension of danger. That more than a hundred men should be killed in one State in a little more than two years, all in substantially the same manner, and that, too, a manner as marked and peculiar as that which characterizes the work of the East Indian Thug; that the victims should all be of one political faith; that from ten to one hundred men should be engaged in each of these homicides, and that no man of them all should be punished for any one of them, may account for the terror with which Southern Republicans have been wont to speak of what the Northern mind has deemed only a grotesque and phantom horror. The mere fact that this number of acts of violence were perpetrated during the time mentioned is, in itself, perhaps of little moment, but the underlying fact that these outrages were but manifestations of a secret force—an organized power whose ramifications extended over a half score of States, and embraced hundreds of thousands of members, and whose emissaries might, at any moment, approach the threshold which a neighbor's hand had marked for their assault—made it terrible indeed. It was the thorough, systematic secrecy of the Society of Jesus, united with the relentless cruelty of the wearer of the cord and creese, which gave to that organization its power in the days of its terrorism, and gives to these crimes now their significance in free America. A thousand men killed in private combats and public broils, from varying motives and in divers manners, are far less terrible to contemplate than a tenth of that number done to death by secret assassination at the hands of disguised emissaries of a hidden power whose secret decree is over and above all law, all the victims being of one class, and slain from a single motive. This was the Ku-Klux organization, and the following are but samples of its work:—

The list of Ku-Klux murders in Georgia, as testified to before the Committee, *gives the names* of fifty-two men killed (one of whom, a negro, was burned alive).

The testimony in regard to each case may be found by refer-

énce to the name under the head of "*Killings,*" in the Index
of Vol. 6, Ku-Klux Reports. 35

In addition to the fifty-two whose names are given, the
report contains accounts of the murders of twenty-two colored
persons, with times and places when they occurred, but without stating the names of those persons, making in Georgia
*seventy-four.*

The list of murders in Alabama, as testified to, gives the
names of *one hundred and nine.* For particulars in each case,
see reference to name in Index to Vol. 8, Ku-Klux Reports. 36

Let no one suppose that the names of all who have been
killed by the Ku-Klux are found in the testimony. These are
only the "killings" *reported under oath* in Alabama, *before*
the investigation of 1872. Other cases are referred to, but the
names not given.

In addition to these there were in Alabama, as shown by the
testimony, one hundred and seventy-nine cases of whipping,
thirty-eight cases of shooting which were not fatal, and sixty
cases of mutilation and other outrages not falling under these
heads. How many victims there were who were not known to
any of the witnesses, or who were afraid to tell what they had
suffered, it would be impossible to guess. It is believed that
not one half the minor outrages were ever revealed.

In Vols. 3, 4 and 5, devoted to South Carolina, are given
one or two lists of names, produced by one witness, which perhaps gives a more vivid idea of the horrors of Ku-Kluxism than
any other single witness could do. The idea that one man could
designate by name so large a number of victims *in one county,*
shows with peculiar vividness the frequency of these outrages,
and give some idea of the terror they must have inspired. On
pp. 919–920 is a list of persons "outraged," and in each case
the kind of outrage is specified. Most of the cases are "whipping" (and further on we shall see some description of this
gentle mode of regulating morals and politics) ; but the list
also includes "Shot—seven wounds," "robbed," "robbed and
threatened," "house broken open," "house burned," [a woman, Charity Blanton] "shot, also her child shot;" "whipped

three times;" "whipped, and his wife driven from home;" " whipped, also his wife;" "whipped and ears cut;" "whipped and shot;" "Jack Surratt, wife, son, and daughter, whipped;" "Ann Bonner and daughter, whipped twice ;" — but this detail is sickening (to read about, at least !). The list includes 227 names, and of these persons, *thirty-eight were women.*

This is probably a good place to see General Forrest's testimony (Vol. 13: p. 9) concerning the copy of the constitution of the original order which he said he had once seen and did not very clearly recall. However, he said :—

" The purport of that constitution, as far as I recollect it now, was that the organization was formed for self-protection. The first obligation they took, if I recollect it aright, was to abide by and obey the laws of the country ; *to protect the weak ; to protect the women and children;* obligating themselves to stand by one another in case of insurrection, or anything of that sort."

This furnishes its own comment.

Besides the foregoing list is another giving the names of 8 men shot to death, 1 man hanged; and all these by bands of disguised men, at night, within a period of about two years. The person who prepared and presented the list was Rev. A. W. CUMMINGS, resident in Spartanburgh since April, 1866, and before that twelve years in North Carolina, one in Tennessee, and before that in Missouri and Southern Illinois ; a clergyman by profession, but during the most of his professional life engaged in educational pursuits, professor of mathematics in one college and president of two others, later.

The manner in which these things are alluded to by the witnesses sometimes gives a better idea of their frequency than could pages of tabulated facts. Hundreds of witnesses speak of murder, mutilation and whipping with that careless insensibility which is born only of familiarity. The following testimony of GRANVILLE BENNETT, a colored man of Alabama, shows that they had ceased to be matter of remark because of their number :—

" Q. You think you have not mentioned all the cases you have heard of from time to time ?

" A. No, Sir; I don't think I have; I know I haven't.

"Q. Have you heard of colored people being whipped ?

"A. Yes, Sir; I have heard of a heap of them being whipped.

"Q. How many, do you think ?

"A. Oh, la ! I couldn't remember them.

"Q. They don't mind that much ?

"A. O no, Sir; *if they can get off with that they can get along.*" (Vol. 9: p. 1730—Ala.)

There are hundreds of such unconscious testimonials to the prevalence of these horrors.

A. B. MARTIN, a white Unionist, seventy-one years of age, who was taken out and terribly whipped in Haralson Co., Georgia, says of the colored people of his county:—

"They whipped them powerfully and have kept whipping them so that they are afraid to come here [to testify before the Committee]. A great many are actually afraid to tell what they know." (Vol. 6: p. 550.)

An exhibition of the same familiarity and *insouciance* is seen in the following :—

"Q. Who did they kill ?

"A. Old man Robin Westbrook.

"Q. Did you ever hear of them committing any other violence ?

"A. Nothing more than just whipping people when they met them; they met them often at night; they waylaid the road for people.

"Q. Did you hear of their whipping many negroes ?

"A. O yes, Sir; I know there has been a great deal of that done about there."

GEO. JONES (colored), Demopolis, Ala.  (Vol. 9: p. 1389.)

Again, we find scores of statements showing that individuals, and even whole communities of those who were the ordinary victims of outrage, "laid out" or slept in the woods, from fear of attack.  We close this chapter with one or two of these.

JOSEPH ADDISON, a native white Georgian, who was whipped and compelled to run away, leaving his stock and crop to those who had driven him off, says:—

"I laid out in the woods *for three weeks from fear of the Ku-Klux.* Then I stayed at home two nights, and on the third they came and took me out and whipped me." (Vol. 6: p. 545.)

J. R. HOLLIDAY, of Jackson Co., Georgia, whose interesting experience will be found more fully stated elsewhere, says:—

" I have three plantations. My hands came to me and told me they were afraid to stay on the plantations. I asked them why, and they said they had seen some disguised men about. I told them they should not be afraid, that I would protect them. Soon after that I found *that my hands had made little hiding-places* (they had dug themselves caves) *in which to stay at night.*"

His wife, ELIZABETH HOLLIDAY, says :—

" The Ku-Klux threatened the negroes on the lower plantation and they were afraid to stay. *They never slept in their houses while they were on the plantation.* (Vol. 6: pp. 415–419.)

## CHAPTER VIII.

### HOSTILITY TO SCHOOLS AND TEACHERS.

IN addition to the political purpose of the Ku-Klux, in most of the States the proceedings were marked by a peculiar development of hostility to free schools, and particularly to free colored schools. The sentiment of the South towards the Northern ladies who went there to teach in the colored schools has been regarded at the North as incredible. They find it hard to conceive that the Christian men and women of the South should have been guilty of such seeming inhumanity and lack of appreciation. And just here the writer desires to pay a well-deserved tribute to that unfortunate class, the "nigger teachers" of the South, since the war. He has known very many of them, perhaps hundreds, and he takes pleasure in here declaring that he has never known a like number of ladies, more accomplished, pure and devoted than the "females" at whom the South sneers. They were usually the daughters of well-to-do families who, inspired with a genuine missionary spirit, determined to give a year or two to the work of enlightening a race whose history had awakened their intensest sympathy. Their social standing at home was uniformly good and in many instances conspicuously so. The daughters of farmers, merchants, college professors and clergymen of the highest eminence were to be found in their ranks. More than one of the most eminent citizens of different States have since chosen noble wives from this devoted band.

It is greatly to be regretted that the good men and women of the South did not cordially receive and co-operate with these worthy and charitably-disposed forerunners of Northern kindliness. That they did not, seems but natural to one who has studied their past and striven to put himself in their places, but it is none the less to be deplored. To the credit of the

Ku-Klux be it said, however, that they rarely interfered with or disturbed these ladies beyond the terror inspired by their mere presence. There were some sad exceptions. The vision of a beautiful corpse—a faithful teacher shot at her post—floats over the page, and the story of flight from a burning school-house, told with white lips even after the lapse of months, comes vividly to the mind of the writer. Yet, even with these, the wonder is that so few of them were molested.

The following shows very clearly and very justly the manner in which they were regarded by that "best class of citizens" to which the witness belonged. His distinctions are peculiarly clear and happy.

CHARLES WALLACE HOWARD, a Presbyterian minister, native of Georgia, sixty years old, editor of "The Plantation," an agricultural paper, Vice President of State Agricultural Society, &c., says:—

"There is a very different condition socially in the estimation placed upon Northern and Southern women at the South. . . . Our women are not inclined to look favorably even upon Northern ladies who come here, so far as their social relations are concerned. . . . They just let them alone. They do not disturb them. I know nothing of the Northern *females* who came to teach colored schools; never spoke to one. They were rigorously excluded from good society." (Vol. 7: pp. 828, *et seq.*—Ga.)

A volume could hardly state it better.

The men who engaged in this missionary work did not fare so easily, either at the hands of the public or the Klan. They seem to have been especial marks for hate and insult on the part of the one and of attack on the part of the other. Some of the instances are too horrible even to relate.

The strongest development of this hostility to schools was probably in Mississippi. The Mississippi State law (after Reconstruction) established separate public schools for white and for colored children, and directed their support as to come from a common school fund consisting of the proceeds of certain land sales, penal fines, license taxes, &c.; and the State Constitution levied in aid of this fund a poll tax, not to exceed

$2 per head, together with taxes for licenses in various kinds of business, and a property tax for building, and one for paying teachers. Both the assessors of these taxes, and the teachers employed, fell under the violent displeasure of the white population. Many of the teachers were "warned" and forced to leave—ladies were visited, threatened and driven away; men warned, visited, whipped, shot and hung—the process apparently being varied according to the stubbornness of the victim, or sometimes in inverse ratio to his power of self-protection.

On this matter may be noted the testimony of Colonel ROBERT W. FLOURNOY (Vol. 11: pp. 82–95): resided in Pontotoc Co., Miss., since 1856; formerly practising lawyer and editor; at present (1871) County Superintendent of Education. Large white county, 52 white and 12 colored schools. Gives various incidents, including K. K. warnings, whippings and killings of teachers of colored schools, and, being asked to what extent visits had been made by men in disguise in that and adjoining counties, replies:—

"They have been riding in that county more or less for the last six or eight months; but of late they have ridden more frequently. There is such a reign of terror there now that persons whose backs are cut all to pieces will actually deny that they have been whipped by them. They are afraid of being killed. These men tell them that if they ever disclose the matter, or say a word about it, they will kill them." (P. 87.)

The case of CORNELIUS MCBRIDE is of interest, as typical of the lighter mode of dealing with such disturbers of the public peace as school-teachers. He was a native of Ireland, twenty-four years of age, had lived and taught school three years in Cincinnati, and afterwards for two years in Mississippi, about a year each in Chickasaw and Aktibbeha Counties. In the latter he taught a public colored school and a white Sunday-school, near the town of Sparta. His testimony may be found in Vol. 11, pp. 325–342. He got on very well for six or seven months, but then began to have warnings in the form of the burning of several school-houses in the neighboring counties;

yet, as he was on good terms with his neighbors and had been selected by them to superintend the white Sunday-school, he did not apprehend much personal difficulty. He was a student, kept quietly at home, took no part in politics, taught colored school every day and two white Sunday-schools on the Sabbath, besides night classes for young men (colored) who could not come to his day school.

In the last week of March, 1871, he was told by some of his scholars that the Ku-Klux were out after him, but paid no attention to it. One night a band of about a dozen men, their faces disguised, with some kind of uniform hat on, and belts, pistols, and bowie knives of uniform pattern, came to the house where he was sleeping, burst in the doors and windows, and presented rifles at him, the leader shouting, "The God damned Yankee, come out here!" He realized the situation, and, determined to escape if he could, leaped through the window between two men with rifles. They caught him, however, struck and beat him with their pistol butts and sheathed knives, and took him off into the fields. He refusing to take off his shirt at their command (he had jumped from his bed), they knocked him down with a pistol and stripped him naked. He thus proceeds in his testimony:—

"Two of them held me down and one of them took a bundle of black-gum switches—a peculiar kind of stick, which stings and raises the flesh where it hits. One of them took the bundle of switches and began to whip me; they said they were going to give me a hundred lashes each. One gave me a hundred; and then another gave me seventy five. I asked them what I had done to merit such treatment. They said, 'God damn you! don't you know that this is a white man's country?' I said the white people were satisfied with my conduct. They have shown it by selecting me to take charge of their Sunday school. They said, 'Yes, damn you, that is the worst thing in it, having a nigger-teacher to teach the white school on Sunday.' I was fighting them all the time, as well as I could—kicking at them and doing what I could—for the torture was horrible. I thought they would kill me any way, when they got through whipping me, and I begged them to shoot me. One of them came up to me with his pistol and asked me if I wanted to be shot. I said, 'Yes;

I can't stand this.' The leader of the party said, 'Shooting is too good for this fellow. We will hang him when we get through whipping him.' I saw a rope hanging from the limb of a tree by the side of the road. There was only one man standing between me and the fence of the plantation. I observed that and tried to gain his attention, for I was determined to make an effort to escape. . . . He was standing between me and the fence and had two pistols. I asked him whether they they would let me off if I would promise to leave in the morning. All this time they were whipping me, but I managed to partly raise myself on my hand and knee. I then made a spring for this man, and struck him as hard as I could. I do not know what part of his body I struck, nor where he went; I know he disappeared and I leaped the fence. As I did so they swore terribly, and fired at me, and the shots went over my head, scattering the leaves all around me. As I went across the field they kept firing at me, and followed me a short distance. . . . It was a very cold night, that night was— piercing cold. I went to the house of a neighbor and friend, Mr. Walser, and remained the rest of the night. Mr. Walser of course sympathized with me. He said, 'My God! has it come to this now, that no man is safe, when you are attacked!' . . . The next day I taught my school as usual." (Pp. 326, 327.)

He taught for several days more, and persisted in holding an examination, which the Ku-Klux had sworn he should not hold—he himself being armed, and several of his white neighbors (who seem to have sincerely respected him and been willing to sustain him) being likewise armed. He slept out in the woods, however, and not long afterwards went to Houston, the county town, to consult with the authorities. He finally went to the Governor, who sent him to the United States District Attorney, and by his aid McBride swore out affidavits against fourteen men, and with a military posse and the United States Marshal proceeded to Sparta to make the arrests. He seems to have shown the traditional valor of an Irishman, and persistent self-protective instinct of a British subject (he had never become a United States citizen).

"When we got to the town of Sparta, Dr. Munson, the Mayor, was asked by the military, "Was not that Joe Davis?" —one of the men I came to arrest. The Mayor sneered at them; said they ought to have photographs of them; he supposed they knew all about the men. He made some sarcastic remarks, and would give no information. In fact, he was the adviser of that whole party." (P. 331.)

The witness gave account of many other similar occurrences —teachers whipped, shot at, driven away; school-houses burned, &c.; especially the case of one Echols, a white teacher of a colored school, who was whipped very badly, and whose case was included in his own, in the arrests he tried to make.

"Q. Has there been any attempt, except this effort made by you, to arrest and punish anybody for any of these crimes you speak of?"
"A. No, Sir; the people are afraid to do it; I was the only one that attempted it, and I risked my life in doing it" (p. 331).

"It is of course understood that these organizations have some political purpose and effect. It is understood that negro men who will vote the Republican ticket are to be punished—shot, hung, or whipped. . . . The colored people talk this way: they say, 'The government has set us free, and *we are worse slaves to-day than in the old slavery times.*'" (P. 332.)

The testimony of this resolute and intelligent young man is of value on other points, namely, the character of the membership and sympathizers with the Ku-Klux Klan in his county (see p. 408), and the trifling reasons given by these disguised "regulators" of social order for inflicting the tortures of the lash on colored men (see p. 433).

One of the most noted cases of their barbarity towards all who attempt to elevate the colored people was that of ELIAS HILL, in South Carolina. He was a remarkable character, a cripple in both arms and legs, a Baptist preacher much respected, and a teacher of the children of his race. He was brutally maltreated and forced to leave. His own testimony is in Vol. 5, pp. 1406–1415.

The same sickening tale is repeated from State after State, and it is utterly impossible to do more here than to give a few thoroughly typical cases. To show that the uncompromising hostility to the free school system (for either whites or

blacks) was not confined to the ignorant or illiterate classes,
we may cite another Mississippi case, that of Col. A. P. HUG-
GINS, as related in his own testimony (Vol. 11: pp. 265–298).    39
A Federal officer through the war, Col. Huggins went in
1865 to Monroe Co., Miss., rented a large plantation, and
until the fall of 1867 was occupied in farming.  He was then
an officer of the Freedmen's Bureau till May, 1869; then assistant assessor of internal revenue; and in March, 1870, County
Superintendent of Schools.  On March 8th he went out some
miles into the country on business of tax assessments and
schools, and on the night of the 9th went to stay by invitation
at the house of a Mr. Ross (hospitality, by the way, for which he
paid, as he says was always his custom there).  That night the
family were awakened by violent rappings at the door, and
demands for the man who was in the house:—

"I stepped to my window and saw that the premises were
completely covered with men dressed in white." . . . After
they had made threats of burning the house, frightening the
family, and throwing the wife of Mr. Ross into spasms, Mr.
Ross begged Colonel Huggins to leave the house, which he
did on the pledge of the leader that he should not be harmed,
as they only wished to deliver to him a "warning."  They
passed down the yard and out of the gate.  "There were one
hundred and twenty in the crowd altogether.  As they passed
out of the gate I numbered them hastily.  The night was as
bright as a moonlight night can well be.  The chief said the
decree of the camp was that I should leave the county within
ten days, and leave the State. . . .  He told me that the rule
of the camp was, first, to give the warning; second, to enforce
obedience to their laws by whipping; third, to kill, by the
Klan all together; and, fourth, if that was not done, and if the
one who was warned still refused to obey, then they were
sworn to kill him, either privately by assassination, or otherwise.  They repeated again that I could not live there under
any circumstances; they gave me ten days to go away, and said
that during that time I must relieve them from all the taxes
of the county. . . .  They said I was collecting taxes from
Southern gentlemen to keep damned old Radicals in office; that
they wanted me to understand that no laws should be en-
forced in that county that they did not make themselves. . . .
There was a white school and a colored school in the neighborhood.  In reference to the white school, they said that they

were not satisfied with it; that they liked Davis well enough as a teacher, but they were opposed to the free-school system entirely; that the whites could do as they had always done before, and could educate their own children; that, so far as the negroes were concerned, they did not need educating at all, only to work. . . . I told them I should leave Monroe County at my pleasure, and not till I got ready. . . . The gate was then thrown open; I was surrounded and disarmed; they took me between an eighth and a quarter of a mile down the road and came to a hill, where they stopped, and asked me if I was of the same opinion, that I would not leave. I told them that I was. I reasoned with them a little; told them that all that I had was there, that this was a very sudden thing, that I would not under any circumstances agree to leave. They ordered me to take off my coat; I refused; they then took it off by force. After that they asked me again if I consented to leave, and I still refused. They then showed me a rope with a noose, and said that was for men like myself who were stubborn; that if I did not consent to go I should die, that dead men told no tales. At this time I saw a man coming from towards the horses, from where I then supposed, and afterwards knew, the horses were. He had a stirrup-strap some inch and a quarter in width, and at least an eighth of an inch thick; it was very stout leather; the stirrup was a wooden one. . . . He came on, and without further ceremony at all—I was in my shirt-sleeves —he struck me two blows, calling out, 'One, two. Now, boys, count!' They counted every lash he gave me. The first man gave me ten blows himself, standing on my left side, striking over my left arm and my back. The next one gave me five blows. Then a fresh hand took it and gave me ten blows; that made twenty-five. They then stopped, and asked me again if I would leave the county. I still refused, and told them that now they had commenced, they could go just as far as they pleased; that all had been done that I cared for; that I would as soon die as take what I had taken. They continued to strike their blows in the same way on my back, until they had reached fifty. None of them struck me more than ten blows, some of them only three, and some as low as two. They said they all wanted to get a chance at me; that I was stubborn, and just such a man as they liked to pound. When they had struck me fifty blows, they stopped again, and asked me if I would leave; I told them I would not. Then one of the strongest and burliest in the crowd took the strap and gave me twenty-five blows without stopping; that made seventy-five. I heard them say 'seventy-five.' At that time my strength gave way entirely; I grew dizzy and cold. I asked for my coat. That is the last

I remember for several minutes. When I recovered myself they were still about me; I was standing; I don't think I had been down; they must have held me up all the time. I heard them say, 'He is not dead yet; he is a live man; dead men tell no tales.' But still they all seemed disposed, as I thought, to let me go. I heard no threatening, except what passed a few moments afterwards. They all passed in front of me, or a great number of them—I will not say all—and drew their pistols, and showed them to me; they told me that if I was not gone within ten days, they were all sworn in their camp, and sworn positively, that they would kill me, either privately or publicly. . . . These men were all armed with the same style of pistol, those that passed before me. Before they got through I had completely recovered my senses, and I noticed everything particularly, and saw that they all had the same style of pistols, what appeared to be about six-inch revolvers. Their clothing I noticed especially; I was with them a long time. [At another place he says, "I was with the Ku-Klux some three-quarters of an hour, I suppose."] It was as light as the moon could make it. Their clothing was all of the same pattern and form; they were all cut and made garments. Their face-pieces were very defective. If I had known the men personally, I could have recognized nearly all of them. I did recognize some of them. . . . Two of them are now under arrest. They lived in that immediate neighborhood. Their names are John S. Roberts and John Porter. Roberts is the son of one who was formerly one of the wealthiest men in the neighborhood. I suppose young Roberts is heir to a plantation of eleven hundred or twelve hundred acres of improved or open land. He is about twenty-five years old. His father is dead. . . . There were no colored men in the band that night. Their hands were not covered. I could see their boots and pants, and I could judge from their hands and feet. Most of them were genteel people, besides being white people. I could also have told by their language if there had been any colored people among them. Their language was that of white men, and cultivated men. . . . In their marching, the three orders I heard were, to Close up; to Keep time; and to Be quiet.

"I wish to state one more thing that both Mr. Ross and myself noticed. We both recognized that they were not drunken men. . . . They took away my pistol, but left it with Mr. Ross for me. They left it for me, and I got it, and have it now. They were not there for thieving—they were not drunken, or anything of that sort, but were merely bent on getting me away. They were a much different class of men from what I ever supposed would meet in a Ku-Klux gang. Of the twenty-eight that are arrested, and are at Oxford, or who were there, the most of them were gentlemanly fellows and well-educated men. . . . They have the captain of the gang, but he was not known to me. He is a young man who lives in the neighborhood, a Willis, a nephew of the man I had stayed with the night before. He is a young man of rather fast habits, but he was not drunk that night. He is a young man about twenty-three or twenty-four years of age, finely educated, and belongs to one of the first families of the county. In all of their proceedings there was perfect order and the most thorough discipline. The little difficulty that was at the head of the column, in pushing me and carrying me along, was the only thing that disturbed the line at all. It was under as fine and as thorough discipline as you ever saw a troop managed in your life. It shows that they had marched before, and knew what discipline was."

The foregoing account is of especial value as being from a man of established character, and of such exceptional courage, coolness, and intelligence that, under these most desperate circumstances, he could see, note, and afterwards clearly describe so many characteristic details of the affair.

A general survey of this feature of the hostility of the Ku-Klux organization to any attempt to educate the blacks—and, indeed, to the entire system of free public schools for white or black—has been made by the Rev. E. Q. FULLER, D. D., editor of the *Methodist Advocate*, Atlanta, Ga. We quote a portion of his article, which, it will be remarked, is simply gathered from the sworn evidence before the Congressional Committee. With this the chapter on Schools will close. He says:—

"The burning of school-houses was a method frequently adopted, a few years ago, to retard or prevent the progress of education among the colored people. The number of houses burned we have no means of ascertaining, but that the Methodist Episcopal Church has suffered seriously from this cause, there is no doubt. A good building at Oxford, Ga., was burned in 1869, under circumstances which clearly pointed to the students of Emory College, of the M. E. Church, South, as complicated with the affair.

"In the testimony of William Jennings, assessor of internal revenue in the Fourth District of Georgia, before the Congressional Committee, he says, in regard to the burning of churches and school-houses, that in 1867–68, such occurrences 'were very common.' 'There was hardly a neighborhood where they were willing to establish colored schools.' 'There are a great many neighborhoods where a colored school would not be tolerated now' (in 1871.)

"Wesley Shropshire, a planter of Chattooga county, Ga., testified that disguised bands came to his place at night and told the negroes that there was an old Radical (Shropshire) on the plantation whom they wanted to see; that the negroes had to vote with the Democratic party; that they (the Ku-Klux) were the friends of the negroes, and the negroes must be friends to them, and if they would do that—vote to please them—they would protect them, but if they would not, they would punish them as they thought proper. A school-house was built on the place for the colored children, and, when nearly completed, the night raiders again made their appearance, and said that they controlled the plantation of Mr. Shropshire, and they would have school-houses when and where they pleased; this one must not be finished; that they would whip the teacher, a colored man, which they did. They left this note for the planter, viz.: 'Mr. Shropshire—Stop this school-house; if you don't, we will be along in a few nights, and give you a hundred licks and burn the house.' The house was not finished, but the colored people, having a church on the same place, commenced a school there under the direction of the State authorities. This house was soon burned, but another was built in its stead, and the school continued.

"Caroline Smith (colored), Walton county, Ga., October 21, 1871, in reply to a question, said: 'Schools! They would not let us have schools. They went to a colored man, whose son had been teaching school, and took every book they had and threw them into the fire, and said they would dare any other nigger to have a book in his house. We allowed last Fall that we would have a house in every district, and the colored men started them. But the Ku-Klux said they would whip every man who sent a scholar there. The school-house is there, but no scholars. The colored people dare not dress themselves and fix up, like they thought anything of themselves, for fear they would whip us. I have been humble and obedient to them—a heap more so than I was to my master, who raised me; and this is the way they serve us.'

"A school-house was burned in the same county in 1868, and one in Warren county about the same time. These points were brought out incidentally in the Congressional investigation, but no effort has been made to get a full report on this question. Not less than twenty churches and school-houses belonging to the Methodist Episcopal Church have been burned in Georgia.

"In Alabama, the condition of things in this particular was no better in those years of confusion—possibly, worse. Dr. Lakin testifies that, in his district, six churches were burned before 1872—four of them within three weeks preceding the election of 1870. He says, also, that many school-houses were burned in North Alabama, and that marked hostility was shown to school-teachers—especially those who taught colored schools.

"White schools supported by Republicans often shared no better fate than those for colored people. William Shapard, Blount County, stopping at Lewis Copland's, was told by that gentleman that a white school taught by Miss Beeson and supported by 'Radicals,' which was commenced on Monday, was broken up on Thursday of the same week. It was again opened in a church, which, in a few days, was burned. Another, in the same county, for whites, taught by Mr. Thompson, was broken up and the house burned because it was supported by Republicans. White persons and native Southerners residing in that county, having agreed to teach colored schools under the county superintendent, were threatened by Ku-Klux and prevented from engaging in this work. Several churches and school-houses were burned in Coosa County; as many, perhaps, in Choctaw County. William Dougherty, of Opelika, testified that, in Macon County, nearly every church and school-house of the colored people was burned. Chambers County was but little, if any, better. The same may be said of other portions of the State.

"Volume 1 of the 'Ku-Klux Conspiracy,' pp. 73–80, gives the situation in Mississippi in 1872. We make the following extracts:

"'In Pontotoc County, the white population largely predominates. There were fifty-two white and twelve colored schools organized. The colored schools employed teachers of a lower grade of qualifications and at smaller salaries than the whites. The most of the teachers employed were natives of the South. Colonel Flournoy, the county superintendent, testifies that, although he made no distinction in politics in employing them, he found, upon inquiry, that of the sixty-four teachers engaged, but eleven were Republicans, and but one of them a colored man.

"'In April and May, 1871, a number of the teachers of the colored schools were called upon by the Ku-Klux and warned that if they did not stop teaching, they would be "dealt with."

" ' A teacher named Smith had been twice called upon, and, after the second visit, abandoned his school, having, as was generally believed, been whipped, although he was too high-spirited to admit it. Colonel Flournoy proceeded:

" ' They said they were determined that there should be no colored schools kept; that they intended to break up every one of them in the State; that it was useless to contend about it; that they should be stopped.

" ' In April, two of the Board of School Directors of Monroe County, who had voted in favor of imposing school tax, were warned by the Ku-Klux to leave the board, and, in pursuance of that notice, one of them did resign. About the same time, all the teachers on the east side of the Tombigbee River, in that county, were notified by them to close their schools, and did so, twenty-six schools thus being interrupted. They went in a body at night and gave these warnings to the teachers.

" ' Among those called upon was a Miss Sarah A. Allen, a young lady sent by a missionary society from Geneseo, Ill., and engaged in teaching one of the free schools. Eighty Ku-Klux came at 12 o'clock on a Monday night, after she had retired, entered her room, and told her she must close her school on Wednesday; that if they came again, she would not get off so easily. She reported this to Colonel Huggins, who says: "Miss Allen made this statement to me herself. She is a highly educated and accomplished young lady."

" ' In April, Rev. Mr. Galloway, a Southern-born man, a Congregationalist, who preached at times to the freedmen, was called upon twice at night by disguised men and notified that he must quit preaching. About the same time, Rev. Mr. Mc-Lachlan, a preacher of the Methodist Episcopal Church, after receiving various warnings, was constrained to leave Oktibbeha County.

" ' The rate of school tax estimated for Monroe County was $10\frac{1}{2}$ mills on the dollar for both buildings and teachers, and the result of the opposition was such that the supervisors were notified that they should not make an assessment, and they did not. Thus, not only were the schools stopped, but the teachers who were driven away were deprived of pay for the time they had taught.

" ' Similar occurrences took place in Noxubee and in Lowndes counties, and so far was it carried in Lowndes County that not only were the schools stopped, but a part of the tax that had been collected was refunded to those who had paid it.' "

This is sufficient to show the drift of sentiment and action on the public-school question at that time. Some subsequent improvement has begun to appear, and will be duly noted.

## CHAPTER IX.

WHAT SOME MEN SAW AND HEARD DURING THESE TIMES.

IN this chapter are grouped the abstracts of testimony taken from a few men of high standing in the comparatively peaceful State of Alabama (Vols. 8, 9, and 10 of the *Reports*). The character and position of these gentlemen, as evidenced by their long-continued residence South, and frequent occupation of places of honor and trust at the hands of their neighbors, will be strong guarantee of their truthfulness and good judgment. The moral of this chapter "points" itself.

Alabama is selected not as furnishing the most numerous or most frequent outrages, but because it was one of the least turbulent of the States; and this is true to such an extent as to give the impression to many persons that the people of that State were not implicated in the Ku-Klux business at all; so that one cannot but exclaim, "If this be done in the green tree, what shall be done in the dry?" The aim of this brief work is only to furnish *examples* from which a fair opinion can be formed. If the object were to make the most horrible effect, the object could be the most easily attained by simply reprinting the seven or eight thousand pages of the K. K. Reports.

Dr. WM. T. BLACKFORD, physician in Greensborough, Ala., from 1857 to 1867; married in that town; Union man before the war; after secession of Alabama tried by a vigilance committee for fidelity to Union, but saved by interposition of friends; served in Confederate army as surgeon without commission, as he would not take oath of fealty to Confederacy; after new constitution of Alabama, under Reconstruction, was elected Probate Judge of his county by 3,520 majority in 1868; held office till about March 1, 1871, when he resigned the position on account of Ku-Klux persecutions, endangering his life.

"Between 1868 and January, 1871, I had received, I think, eleven different notices from the Ku-Klux organization to leave the county, or that they would 'go for' me. . . . The first one was a printed circular. 'It is ordered by'—I cannot begin to go over it. It went over a lot of rigmarole of 'grand cyclops' and 'caverns and shadows of death,' and a lot of bombast rolled up into the form of an order. The substance was that I must leave the county at once, or that when they came their mission was blood, etc. . . . I then received a letter on or about the 4th of July, 1868, addressed to me, on which there was a picture resembling that on the strychnine bottles in drug stores, which is two thigh bones crossing each other immediately under a naked skull, and written under that 'Behold what you will be in a few days,' or 'Behold your doom in a few days,' and then went on stating, 'If you remain,' etc., 'what you may expect.' I was not a 'carpet-bagger,' but a 'scalawag'—a native who had taken office under the new constitution. The Ku-Klux proclaimed that no man should hold office where he was elected by negroes; that it was not the representation of the people, but of the usurpation of the government power that had conferred upon a lot of damned monkeys and baboons the right of suffrage, and as a people they would not submit to it, and that was the object of the organization of the Ku-Klux, or one of its objects. . . . I was connected by marriage with one of the first families in the county, every one of the members of which was of the Democratic persuasion. Everything I had in the world was right there and had been accumulated there. I had given four years of service in my medical capacity to the Confederate Government, and there was no ground whatever of opposition to my holding office except the single one that I was a Republican and held office under the new constitution. . . . I had some horses—fine horses—stock, and the boys had been giving me a good deal of trouble opening my stable doors, shooting my dogs, etc. They had several times entered my stable and carried my trotting wagons and sulkies away off to the Southern University and put them up on the balconies, and such things—all of which I looked on as harmless sport. Four or five months before the Ku-Klux visit of January, 1871, a gentleman of prominence in the State of Alabama, a Confederate general, who is personally a warm friend of mine, came to me and asked me to resign. He stated that I would not be permitted to hold the office of Probate Judge any longer, and that in order for my personal security I had better resign, and do it peacefully and quietly, and leave the county. . . . No objection had been made to the manner in which I had administered the affairs of the office.  On the contrary, every attorney in that town asserted that I was—to use their expression—'one of the best officers that they ever saw.'  On the night of the 19th, 1871, there was a body of disguised men, about sixty or seventy, visited Greensborough. They went to the house of my mother-in-law, Mrs. L. M. Nutting, and demanded entrance.  . . .  They inquired for me, tore up the clothing in my room, searched every nook and corner in the house, and failing to find me, went to a suite of rooms that I had in the building where my office was.  . . . They failed to find me.  . . .  They passed on down the street by Mrs. Nutting's.  They stopped opposite the house and fired a number of shots into the house, one of which passed through the window into my little daughter's room, of between eleven and twelve years of age; she was sleeping with her grandmother.  They did not miss her by more than six or eight inches.  While they were ransacking Mrs. Nutting's I was informed by a negro and escaped from my rooms in the office, left my bed, and with what clothes I could grab in my hands (a coat and pair of breeches, though I was barefoot) I escaped to the woods."

He lay out in the woods for seven nights, coming into town by day, but being warned by negroes and their friends (some respectable white men) that the nights were not safe for him;—seven nights with no shelter at all, and eight or nine either in negro cabins or sleeping in the woods with a few faithful negroes guarding and watching for Ku-Klux.  This in cold, rainy, frosty weather in January.

Then he complained to the Governor of the State, and some talk was made about protecting him, but it all resolved itself into his being advised by a committee of the best and most influential men in the town (one editor, one professor in the University, and others of like high standing) that his life was not safe; they regretted it, but could not help it, and he had better go.  They arranged to purchase his property (at less than it had been bought for at auction in 1867), and, sending off a few horses to Kentucky, he finally left the place, being escorted to the cars by some ten or twelve armed negroes.  Men whom he represents as his nearest friends and most efficient advisers at this time were Democrats of high consideration and standing, who, despite their warm friendship, could only advise him to go, and could not protect him.

In reference to the general existence of the Ku-Klux organization in Alabama, Dr. Blackford testifies :—

"During the time between their visit to me in January and my leaving for Kentucky, there was a Confederate General, a warm personal friend of mine, who took me into his room at the hotel at Greensborough, and remarked to me, in the course of his conversation, 'This organization is thorough in these negro counties, as much so as it can be.' He went on and named Hale, Greene, Tuscaloosa, Sumter, and all the south-western counties that were largely populated with negroes ; that the organization had—I forget the exact amount, but it seems to me he stated $500,000, in its treasury; that the capitation tax on each member was 50 cents per week, and that they had their county organizations and their district organizations; that the districts were presided over by a superior officer, and they had their State organization ; that they had expended a large amount of money for police duty; and that the object of the organization was to put down negro suffrage.

"He stated to me that he had organized the Ku-Klux of Arkansas, and what they had done. He told me about the blowing up of the steamer that was sent to carry arms to the State of Arkansas—something that I had never heard of. He said it was done by the authority of that Order. I asked him what was its extent throughout Alabama. He said in reply, 'It is better organized than ever the Confederate army was.' And he stated that in all these negro counties they had resolved to carry the elections, and that in connection with that they intended to force and compel every officer that was now holding office to resign, or they would dispose of him, and added, 'You are going through what the rest of the Republican officers will be compelled to go through.' I said to him, 'Have these organizations no fear of the General Government ?' He replied, 'Not at all, because they control juries;' they had *members already in the United States Congress ;* they had members in the Legislature of the State; they had members that they could at any time prove an *alibi,* or that every jury had more or less of them on it, and that so long as the government remained in its present form they were perfectly secure; that they had members of their organization in the Union League; that they had put them in there for the purpose of ascertaining what was done; and detectives, police, and plenty of means to carry out anything that they proposed. He then stated, 'Now, to show you how this thing is conducted; I do not think there was any person that waited on you that lived in your county, but when the Council meets, and they propose to dispose of you here in this county, they will call upon the Klan in another county to go and attend to that, and perhaps but one or two of the members of the organization in your county will know anything about it, and they will only know it in order to point out where you stay.' He told me that this organization was first organized in Tennessee. Of course he did not communicate any signs or pass-words. He said that when certain parties had violated the obligation, they were taken by the Klan and disposed of." (Vol. 9: pp. 1271–1283.)

SAMUEL F. RICE. Practising lawyer in Alabama since 1838; in Montgomery, Alabama, since 1852; several times member of the State Legislature, both House and Senate; at one time public printer to the State; afterwards Judge and Chief Justice of the Supreme Court. Practises in many counties, and has large general acquaintance throughout the State:—

"I have heard of Ku-Klux outrages in several parts of the State, not many parts. I do not think this Ku-Klux organization exists in many counties of the State. I have no idea that it is anything else than political in its character, and it always operates in the interest of the Democratic party. It grew out of the passions and hates engendered at the beginning of the late war and subsisting at its termination, which are now diminishing in force with a large number, but with too many are not abated at all. From the best information I have, there are in the organization respectable, clever men, who, aside from this, would be accounted first-class men anywhere. What I mean to say is, I am satisfied the organization is not confined to any low order of people. I believe that good men —men in every other respect free from objection—belong to it. I think that one of their main objects is to annul practically that feature of the Reconstruction policy which gives to the colored men the free exercise of the right of suffrage. You may group the whole matter, I think, by saying that the object is to deprive the Republican party, not only of political rule, but of any force or respectability in the State. From what I have heard colored men say, I am satisfied that a good many of them have absolutely abstained from the right of suffrage because they were afraid of the violence threatened by such organizations." (Vol. 8: pp. 518–519.)

E. WOOLSEY PECK. Has resided in Alabama forty-eight years; in Tuscaloosa since December, 1833. Chief Justice

Supreme Court. Before the war was practising lawyer, and for a time Chancellor. Was a Union man, opposed to secession. Never received any personal injury, but was hung in effigy and suffered many indignities; was warned to leave the State, but refused:—

"My opinion is, from observation and other means of information, that the criminal laws of the county, especially in relation to many crimes, and that class of people who engaged in the late Rebellion, have not been executed; and in my opinion they cannot be, with the present sentiments and feelings of the people—that offenses committed cannot be punished by courts and juries. The ordinary offenses perhaps may be, but not even those, with a certain class of people. The special class of offenses that the courts cannot reach are those violences which have been committed upon the people by those who are most violent in their feelings and prejudices against the Government, such as murders, whippings, threatenings, &c. (Vol. 10: p. 1851.)

"The *purpose* of the Ku-Klux organization I do not know, but it has the *effect* either to drive from the county or from their neighborhood a great many men. It seems mostly to have been directed against the colored population. It has also had, I believe, the effect to deter negroes from voting, and I am perfectly persuaded that the main object of the order is to obtain for the Democratic party the political control of the State (p. 1856).

"I believe that if the Democrats were to combine and earnestly endeavor to put down these outrages, they could be stopped, because I believe that those generally who do the actual mischief are the inferiors, who are operated upon by higher spirits, that are not so open and manifest to the world. I believe that in Tuscaloosa County, in Hale and Greene counties—I speak now from information, and not from personal knowledge—that a very large proportion, a very large majority, of what are called the Democratic people in those counties, either actually belong to or sympathize with what is called the Ku-Klux Klan. . . . I feel it my duty to say that there are a great many good men among Democratic people who I do not believe sympathize with the Ku-Klux organization—a great many. But my fears are that a majority of those who are called Democrats do sympathize with it, and many of the most intelligent of them are members of that body, and are the managers and controllers of the mischief that is done through its instrumentality." (Vol. 10: p. 1857.)

## CHAPTER **X.**

### SHORT STORIES FROM THE NEW "BOOK OF MARTYRS."

THE following cases have been selected as illustrative of different points which have been made in the foregoing pages.
The careful reader will find here cases the facts of which more
than parallel the most vivid pictures in "A Fool's Errand,"
and he will perceive that, instead of being magnified, the incidents of that narrative have actually been modified only by
an alleviation of their horrors. It should be remembered that
the narratives which follow are but brief statements of the
facts appearing in evidence before the Congressional Committee, uncontradicted and undeniable, reference being given
to the pages of the Reports where the testimony may be found.
They are valuable as exponents of the social and moral life in
which they existed unpunished, unhindered, and only "*deplored* by the best people of the South" when some gust of
angry denunciation came from a half-incredulous North. One
of the uses of all noxious weeds is to show the character of
the soil in which they grow, and some of the most noisome
mark the richest soil when once it shall be reclaimed from
savagery.

### PERRY JEFFERS.*

Perry Jeffers was a Georgia slave. At the time of the
emancipation he had lived to a good old age, but still being
vigorous in body he hoped to enjoy for a number of years the
sweets of liberty with his family. He had seven sons, all of
whom, save one, were strong, industrious, dutiful, and promising for a life of usefulness and prosperity. One was an invalid
and helpless from birth, rendered so by prenatal injury to the

* This narrative is from the pen of the able editor of the *Methodist Advocate*, Atlanta, Ga., the Rev. E. Q. Fuller, D.D.

slave mother by accident or otherwise. She, at the time the events here narrated took place, had wholly failed in health, and, under the burdens of that horrible system, had become greatly enfeebled.

But at last freedom came to them, bringing new hope and promising a future rosy with visions of home and happiness. Never before had these men gone to the cotton-fields with such light hearts and quickened paces. Never before had they gathered around the humble hearthside to talk of coming years with gladsome voice and interludes of joyous song. Farms, homes, and the comforts of life danced before their excited fancy. The highest of their ambition was to acquire an education, to read books and papers, to become familiar with the thoughts of the good and the great in the present and past ages. The hope of becoming *men* and of being recognized as such among their fellows stirred their souls to the depths of their being.

But these anticipations were kindled only to be quenched in untimely and violent death. The Ku-Klux watched their movements and haunted them in their dreams. They left them neither day nor night in the unmolested enjoyment of the blessings which God had given and their industry had acquired. Well directed labor and rigid economy had begun to bring their accustomed rewards to this household. But these virtues, which in other lands would have won respect and position, only awakened envy and malice among those around them. It was often said of them that they sold too much cotton, bought too much stock, had too much money, were far too independent; that if they continued in this way a few years they would get ahead of the white folks. But few had better credit in Augusta with the merchants of the city. And then, worst of all, they had books, and the young men had learned to read and to keep accounts. They were getting above their business and social position and must be taught to "know their place." Free "niggers" were dangerous unless they were made to respect white people. They were living at this time, in 1868, on the Brinkley plantation near Camac, in Warren County, Ga.

This was their old home, Mr. Brinkley, brother-in-law of Judge Gibson, of Augusta, having been the owner of this family. By his kindness, forethought, and the just treatment of his former slaves he still held their confidence, and made it profitable both to himself and them to rent them the whole plantation. But neither his influence in the community nor interest in their welfare afforded protection in the time when that was most needed.

One Thursday night early in November the light had gone out upon the hearth, had in fact been put out earlier than was wont, books were laid aside, song was hushed, laughter suppressed, and conversation carried on in low tones or whispers, for warning had been given by a friend that the Ku-Klux had determined to make them "know their place." At the midnight hour one on watch peering out between the logs, of which the house was built, saw a person robed in white pass through the gate, and then another, and another, till a large company, having the feet of their horses muffled, had stolen in silently as the tread of death, and stood in ghastly array like ghosts from the regions of the lost. Hark! what was that? A flash, and the crack of shot-guns from within the house. The inmates had not been sleeping, but watching. These ghouls from the moon, or spirits of the Confederate dead, as they called themselves, were evidently sensible to powder and lead. One fell in mortal anguish, and three others were wounded. The fallen were quickly gathered up, and the regulators hastily withdrew.

Such audacity on the part of colored men had never been known before. Had they a right to defend their homes? The popular verdict was against them. The white people said emphatically, No! Black men had no rights which white men were bound to respect. They must be punished, aye, killed. To leave one alive, it was claimed, would be to invite insurrection and slaughter of the whites. They had killed a white man and the family must perish. Besides this, the one slain was a member of the Ku-Klux Klan, and by a law of that order any one who should kill, though in self-defence, or, as in

this case, in the protection of home, one of their number, must
be put to death, and all members of the order were under solemn obligations to assist, if called upon to do so, in inflicting
this penalty.  This law of the Ku-Klux was also in harmony
with the sentiment of the people, and these " ghouls," as General
Forrest says they were designated, were expected to execute
the common behest.  During the two nights following they
prowled around what was once the home of Perry Jeffers, from
which he and his six sons were compelled to flee because they
had dared to defend themselves in this sacred retreat.  Their
lives had been declared forfeited by that act which in any
other land, by any other people, would not only have been justified by the facts, but applauded as brave, chivalrous, and
noble.

The week waned.  The holy Sabbath dawned, but it was not
a day of peace to the community, nor to the terrified fugitives
hiding from the vengeance of their fellow-men like the frightened hare from pursuing hounds.  At the church, around the
fireside, and everywhere that neighbors met, the one topic of
conversation was the Jeffers'.  They must be hunted, punished, slain.  Doxologies had been sung in the house of God and
benedictions from the Father of Mercies solemnly pronounced
in the name of the Prince of Peace upon those who were then
swearing to wreak vengeance upon these flying, frightened
freedmen.  But no song, nor prayer, nor blessing, nor thought
of mercy was indulged for them, who were in the greatest
need of help and protection.  In the darkness of night, like
the lynx after its prey, the white-robed demons again surrounded the home of Perry Jeffers.  He had not returned nor
been seen in the neighborhood since the fatal night.  Disap-
pointed again, these human ghouls seized his helpless boy,
dragged him from his bed out into the night, and shot him to
death.  They took also the aged and infirm mother—these were
the only inmates found in the house—and with a bed-cord
hung her to a tree in the yard.  While this was being done,
others took all of the articles of household furniture from the
cabin, piled them upon the body of the dead boy and set them

on fire, and by this light these so-called Christian men in this so-called Christian land retreated to their homes and to the enjoyment of peaceful slumbers.

The former master, Mr. Brinkley, living near by, ran to the aid of the old lady, cut the rope and saved her life, though at the cost of untold suffering and more intense anguish over her dead. Dr. Darden, of Warrenton, who was murdered in the following March, commenced an inquest over the charred body of this helpless victim, but as the facts were being evolved he was ordered by the Ku-Klux neighbors to cease. They said: "This thing has gone far enough; it must be closed up." Thus ended the investigation, and the half-burned remains were buried by night in secret, where they await the resurrection of the just to confront in the great day the actors in these crimes.

Meanwhile Perry Jeffers and his six sons had fled to Warrenton, the county seat, and sought protection from the sheriff of the county, J. C. Norris, Esq., who had espoused the Union cause and was doing heroic work in behalf of the reconstruction of the State and in the maintenance of peace and order in society. There being no persons in the jail at the time, Mr. Norris kept them concealed there for several days till it became evident that the frenzy of the Ku-Klux was so great that they could not live in that section. It was decided to send them to South Carolina, and on the 9th of November, 1868, they were put on the train at Warrenton for Augusta. R. C. Anthony, agent of the Freedmen's Bureau, went with them four miles to the junction at Camac and put them on the train on the main line of road in the special care of the conductor. At Dearing, eighteen miles from Camac and twenty-nine miles from Augusta, on the Georgia Railroad, the place where Senator Adkins left the train when he was murdered, the father and five sons were taken from the car, at about twelve o'clock in the day, and shot to death, the perpetrators of the deed not being at the time disguised or in any way concealed. That was not necessary, as these willful and wicked murders were justified by the people on the ground that the Jeffers' had killed a white man who was a Ku-Klux. The youngest son alone escaped, and is left the sole representative of the family. Such was the boon of freedom to Perry Jeffers.

Before the Congressional Committee, Mr. Norris testified that this family were as "respectable colored people as you will find anywhere." Said he, "The old man was one of the most industrious men I ever saw. He was a good farmer and was making money." "Was there any charge against them?" asked Mr. Poland. "No charge in the world," was answered. "Was any thing pretended against them?" "No, sir, nothing was pretended that I ever knew. The former owner of this old man, Mr. Brinkley, said he was as good a man as he had ever seen in his life. When a slave he never had any trouble with him." Within a few months after this, shot-guns and revolvers were taken by force from colored men so as to make it safe for Ku-Klux to carry on their operations. This is one reason why they have done so little in self-defence.

(See testimony of different witnesses, Vols. 6 and 7 (Ga.), pp. 209, 210, 211, and 1029.)

## J. R. HOLLIDAY.

This white native of Jackson County, Georgia, was a man of a different type from the former slave, Jeffers—a type little known and hard to be understood by men of Northern birth, because such men have no place in the ideal South, which has an existence only in Northern minds. He was a Southern man, born and raised in the county. The father was a poor man, who died when Holliday was still young, and the widow being ill able to support her numerous family, the young Robert was apprenticed to a millwright. He grew up strong, industrious, and sturdy, taking life in a resolute, tireless way, which, when he reached the age of forty-one, found him the owner of three valuable plantations and still carrying on at times the trade to which he had been reared.

He did not live in a grand mansion: a modest, ungraceful frame wooden house, with its wide hall stretching through the middle, and that superabundance of porch which abounds among his class, still served as his home. It was a low-eaved, brown, dull-looking house, but then Robert Holliday had promised his daughter, then fifteen, that she should be married from as fine a house as Jackson County had in its limits. He had not yet begun its erection, as he had not decided how he would divide out his three broad plantations among his children. In truth he clung to his old home even as he clung to his old life, from which his wealth and success were daily taking him further away. So the house was enlarged and repaired as the family grew larger and time made rents and crannies through which the wind and the storm came in, though he was one of the richest men in his county, having strictly obeyed the injunction, "owe no man anything."

This man J. R. Holliday, farmer and millwright, lived in his house and was only "Bob" Holliday to his former lordly neighbors. But he still worked, and was careful, temperate and frugal, and grew richer; while they were reckless and extravagant, and grew poorer as a consequence. Besides, they were, like nearly all Southern men of reputed wealth when the war broke out, overburdened with debt. Had it not been for the bankrupt law of 1867, it is difficult to say what would have become of the Southern people. Had it not been enacted and the old law allowing imprisonment for debt been continued in force, some of those who now roam about the halls of Congress must have been content with a "debtor's room" in the common jail. It is one of the material benefits flowing from the legislation attending Reconstruction for which the nation has received little credit and no loving gratitude from these men themselves.

One morning in the spring of 1871 Bob Holliday went early to his "river plantation," three miles away, and when just at daylight he rode up and hailed the group of huts which constituted his "lower" or "river" plantation, he found the houses of his colored people not only closed but empty. After a while his call was heard and one after another of his twenty odd hands came forth from some place of concealment. "What does this mean?" asked the impetuous owner. Then he was

told, somewhat fearfully, for they knew not but that he was
one of the Klan, that the Ku-Klux had been there, had taken
away their guns, had whipped some and had threatened others;
that from fear of a repetition of this visit they had "slept out"
ever since, at first in the woods and bushes and then in little
caverns which they had dug for themselves along the second
banks of the river. At this recital Mr. Holliday was wroth.
He did not care so much for the suffering and terror of the colored people as he did for the affront and injury which was
done to himself. These men were in his employ, "*his niggers*,"
he said, at work on his plantation, under his direction and
control, and in a certain sense under his protection. He would
not have his affairs thus interfered with. So he berated the
poor colored men furiously, and yet not unkindly, and bade
them return to their cabins and live and sleep in them hereafter. If they were in any manner molested or interfered with,
they were to let him know and he promised to protect them.

It was not long before one of them had some trouble with a
young white man of the neighborhood, and Mr. Holliday be-
friended him so far as to stand his bail when accused of as-
saulting his persecutor, and to employ counsel in his behalf.
Then his plantation was again raided and his hands driven off,
some taking to the woods and their dens again, and others coming to live at his house and walking back and forward to and
from their daily toil. The sturdy self-made man chafed under
this state of affairs, and made some threats—uttered some defi-
ance to the Klan. The time came when he was called on to
make good his words. But he shall tell the story of that night
in his own way, as he gave his testimony before the sub-committee in Atlanta on the 21st of October, 1871:—

"One night, about eleven o'clock, Prince McElharmon sent
me word that I had better keep my eyes skinned that night. I
sent off and got a gallon of spirits to treat my hands with. I
moved from my wife's room into another bed-room. There
were four rooms on that floor of the house, a cook-room, dining-
room, and bed-room, and one where I and my wife slept.
About eleven o'clock I heard my dog bark. I will say that I
had heard threats all the year, but I thought they did it to ag-

gravate me because I opposed the Ku-Klux party, and showed
them the law, and told them that it was injurious to our State
for them to act that way, and that it would fetch our State
into trouble; that it was a bad thing and a dangerous thing.
I explained the whole law to them, but it looked like it aggra-
vated them.    At eleven o'clock that night I heard my dog
bark.    I peeped out of the window and I saw some disguised
men coming in my gate.    They were not ten steps off, and
probably there were betwixt twenty and thirty of them.    I
shot right into a pile of them.    I had nothing but duck-shot
in my gun.    My pistol was on the mantel-piece.    I had a drill-
sword that belonged to my brother.    My brother was captain
of that district during the Confederate war.    When I shot a
portion of them dispersed.    Some rushed one way and some
another.    One man came rallying the crowd; he was about
three parts drunk, and ran into the cook-room, hollering,
'Come on, boys.'    I did not know which door they would
come in at.    I went to the back room where my wife slept, and
I saw through the crack of the door some parties whom I
knew and whom I recognized.    One of them says, 'Let's run
in here; they are fighting in the cook-room.'    I saw that the
whole crowd was going to gather there, and I went to the door
of the dining-room.    One of them had an ax in a belt around
him.    This fellow ordered the door to be cut down.    I was
standing by the side of the door with a gun, and as they came
in I knocked down some two or three men, or three or four of
them.    Then it seems as if I struck a little too high and hit
the top of the door, for I broke my gun.    I was in my shirt-
sleeves and bareheaded and barefooted.    I then got out this
knife [taking from his pocket a large knife].    While I was
getting it out they ran in and covered me all over, and struck
my head with a pistol.    Then they cut me on this knuckle
[pointing to it].    The first man I cut I stuck my knife right in
here [pointing his finger over the region of the heart].    The
other man I cut a little higher up, I do not know exactly
where, and the third one I cut I do not know exactly how.
We fought there until the crowd was pretty much dispersed
out of the room.    The reason I was saved was this: I had a
colored man there who was very much scared; he got a light,
as he was coming in behind them with the light I could see
them and they could not see me.    One of them said, 'Take
care, boys; let me shoot him.'    That was after I had pretty
much whipped the crowd out with my knife.    Then two of
these fellows followed me, shooting at me; they fought clear
from the dining-room all through the bed-room and into my
wife's bed-room, and they shot into the facing of the door,

They were so scared that that is the way, I think, that kept them from killing me. I then unbolted the back-room door and went out, for I saw there was no sense in my fighting men with my knife when they all had pistols. I went out into the orchard and lay down there a minute to see which way the crowd was going. I thought I would go over the hill and get a double-barreled gun and meet them there and kill them; but I found that the road was picketed. I recognized a portion of the men.

"Q. Did you next morning see any sign of any injury having been done by your cutting or shooting ?

"A. I looked, but I saw nothing but bullet-holes and some blood on my knife. I was mad, and fretted and pestered in such a manner that I did not take much time to look. There was a little blood on my forehead. A great many parties came in and there was a great deal of confusion and excitement.

"Q. What was your course during the war ?

"A. I opposed Secession *in toto.* During the war I staid at home and attended to my mills myself. I attended to all the wants of the people, even to the wives of the soldiers, and took care of my old mother, who had no protector whatever there. I built water-wheels for factories, etc.

"Q. What has been your course since the war ?

"A. As a general thing I have taken no political stand, no more than I have opposed fighting against the Government. As a general thing I have spoken against any set of people being lawless, or doing anything contrary to the Government. I said that the best thing that the people could do was to behave themselves; that the Government would give them all their rights if they would only behave themselves and show themselves loyal people and not a rebellious people.

"Q. You have taken no active part in politics since the close of the war ?

"A. No, sir; I do not think I have voted but once since then, because I did not think there was much use in voting the way they were going on, and from what I could see of the general feeling of the people; and, more than that, I did not think the Government would find much use spending money here unless we have the right kind of men to try these cases before them."

This rugged, sensible man was compelled finally to leave his home, though he contemplated returning again. Their story, as told by himself and his equally brave and resolute wife, is to be found at pages 414 and 417 of Volume 6 of the *Ku-Klux Reports.*

### JOE AND MARY BROWN.

Joe and Mary Brown were colored people, who lived in White County, Georgia. Joe's "ole missus" had told him in the old slave time that he was born "in the year thirty," and that was all he knew of his age. He had the reputation of being "a good, likely nigger" in those days and continued to maintain that character afterwards. He was more thrifty and prudent than many of his race, and on that account was regarded as quite a catch among the dusky belles along the river, until Mary, a comely, ebon lass of some twenty years, made him her bondsman by marriage. She was sprightly and bright, given to quick replies and pleasant jest; but he was of a more serious turn, as became the head of a household.

They lived thriftily, worked hard, and, despite two young lives which were born into their care, had gathered enough together by the spring of 1869 to buy and pay down the cash for a little farm of about forty acres with a small cabin upon it. A white man wanted it, but Joe outbid him by twenty dollars and got the land. He had no idea that this was an offence, and even felt a bit of natural pride that he, "a poor nigga turned loose wid only his claws, at de close ob de wah," should be able to outbid a white man who had "been his own master ever since he was man grown," as he was wont to tell his friends in recounting this notable feat. He little thought that it was a crime and an insult to his white neighbors.

His wife's mother, a younger sister, two children, and an orphan girl who nursed them while their mother worked in the crop, and a decrepit father made up their household. They worked hard, managing to cultivate the little farm and yet have many unemployed days to work for their white neighbors. They were healthy, happy, and full of hope.

One day Mary was going to a neighbor's in the bend of the river below. Instead of going the longer way around by the public road she went across the fields. It was midsummer, and the corn grew rank and close in the river bottoms. She went on singing merrily between the corn-rows. Then she was silent, and her unshod feet made no noise upon the soft ground.

All at once she came upon two men with guns in their hands, who sprang aside when they saw her and stood watching her two or three corn-rows off. Their faces were black, but in the hasty glance she had she saw the white skin beneath their shirt-collars and around their wrists. She was of a quick, fearless nature, and, though greatly frightened, she knew at once that her best way was to pass by as if she had not seen them. She did so, and they watched her silently as she passed on. When she was out of sight she gathered up her skirts and ran. She reached the end of the field out of breath and ready to laugh at her own fright. Just as she did so, a girl of their acquaintance came up and asked her why she had been running, and received a saucy laughing reply as to some one she had seen in the corn-field. She at once began to tease the new-comer in regard to a colored man of her acquaintance.

While they stood talking together they heard two shots fired from the place where she had seen the two white men disguised as colored men, and presently two more: a deputy United States Marshal, named Cason, had come across the river in a boat and was shot as he stepped ashore. Mary reflected that it would be safest for her to keep her own counsel, though she knew both of the men, and the body lay not more than forty steps from where they had stood, just at the left of the private cross-ing used by Cason and a few other neighbors. So she held her peace. A short time afterwards a white woman in the neighborhood, the wife of a prominent planter, asked her what she had been telling about two young men (naming the ones she had seen in the corn-field) having killed Mr. Cason. She said she had not told any one such a thing. A day or two af-terwards some neighbors told her little son, about five or six years old, to tell his parents that they could not live there any more, and if they did not leave in five days they would kill them. The parents laughed at the threat, for the terrors of the Klan were not yet fully appreciated and they thought it a silly attempt of some drunken gentleman to terrify "a little nigger." Secure in conscious innocence, they apprehended no danger. The husband and wife and the still vigorous mother worked

on.   The decrepit father hobbled down to the river each day
and patiently fished in order that he might do something toward the support of the busy hive in which he dwelt.

Upon these scenes of industry, peace, and happiness came
the Ku-Klux.   It was about two or three o'clock in the morning, and the tired inhabitants of the humble domicile were in
the soundest slumber, when there came a sudden rush of shouting and infuriate men.   The doors were broken down, the
chinking torn out from between the logs, and the muzzles of
numerous guns and revolvers thrust in, before the affrighted
sleepers could realize what was being done.   Joe, who had retired before the others, sprang to his feet and gazed about him
in affright.   One after another arose, and by the firelight which
they compelled him to kindle on the hearth the masked ma-
rauders counted them.   "Where are the rest?" they cried.
"You were all here at dark, and we are going to kill all of
you.   We don't mean for any to get away."   Then, still cover-
ing poor Joe with their firearms, they made him bring out into
the yard a brand and required him to make up a bright fire.
Then the others were brought out of the house, one after
another, and ranged in line before the fire, Mary being the last
one dragged from her place of concealment.   Then the work
for which they had come began.   Joe Brown was stripped entirely naked and thrown on his face upon the ground.   One of
the crowd stood upon Joe's head while he was beaten by the
others with the long tough reed fishing-poles which the old man
used, and with hickory whips, until from sole to crown there
was hardly a place which did not bear the mark of a blow.

Then the wife was stripped in like manner, and beaten until
she was almost insensible.   A chain was put around Joe's neck,
and he was dragged about the yard, naked and bleeding, in
sheer wantonness of savage sport.   In the midst of her torture
the wife cried out to know why she was thus tortured.   They
said, "What is that you are going down to Atlanta to swear
against?"   "Nobody," she replied.   Then they pulled her up
by a trace-chain about her neck, and gave her twenty-five or
thirty more lashes, and repeated their question, only to get the

OLD UNCLE JOE CATCHING A DINNER.

same answer. Then they asked who she had seen down the river the day Cason was killed, and she replied, Bailey Smith and Frank Hancock. They said they had come to whip her about that, and she told them that she had never mentioned it to a soul before that time. Then she was knocked down with a pistol for her impudence in pretending to deny it, beaten again with hickories, and finally choked with the log-chain until she was insensible. Then, as some of the softer-hearted of the thirty odd masked "patrol" objected to absolute killing, water was thrown over her until consciousness returned, and she was allowed to drag her naked, bleeding form along the ground to the fire, while they turned their attention again to her husband.

The words in which the old mother tells this are touching indeed. She says:—

"They beat him with long sticks, and wore out a long fishing-pole on him. They had him down, and put a chain on his neck, and dragged him about a good deal. Joe said, "I ain't done anything, gentlemen; what are you abusing me for?" They said, "We will kill you, God damn you. You shall not live here." He said, "I have bought my land, and got my warrantee title for it; why should I be abused in this way?" They said, "We will give you ten days to leave, and then, God damn you, we will burn your house down over you, if you don't go."

Having thus beaten the husband and wife, they now turned their attention to the rest of the family, who were whipped, though less cruelly. Then they stripped all the females—the old mother, Caroline Benson, her daughter Rachel Arnold, the young colored girl Mary Neal, and the little daughter of Joe Brown, and compelled them all to lie down beside the naked and bleeding Mary Brown, while they offered them still further indignity, and enacted a hideous orgy of shame in the dim light of the swift-coming summer morning.

Mary and Joe were both for a time near the brink of the grave from their injuries. Said the former, pathetically, "I shook like an ague for four days." It was two weeks before Joe could leave the house. As soon as they were able to move they fled, leaving to their persecutors all that could not be removed. It seems terrible, but Joe was thrifty, and, consequently, an "impudent nigger," and poor Mary had been the unwilling observer of a Ku-Klux murder. As for the other women exposed to nameless indignities—why, they were not treated as badly as they might have been, though it was perhaps rather rude sport for gentlemen. It was not the same as if they had been white women, though, and they had not so much reason to complain, since they fared so much better than many of their neighbors. No doubt they were all glad to get off as lightly as they did. Even Joe and Mary may easily have known of those who were far worse off than they.

The testimony of Joe Brown, Mary Brown, Caroline Benson, and Mary Neal, giving full and detailed accounts of this frolic, together with the names of many of the gentlemen engaged in it, which have been here omitted, may be found on pages 375, 386, 388, and 501 of Vol. 6, *Ku-Klux Reports.*

JOHN L. COLEY (white), of Huralson Co., Ga., who was ku-kluxed for having sold a pistol to a negro, gives this account:—

"They took me out by the side of the road, and to a shade-tree, where they hanged me up by the neck, pulled me up clear from the earth. The last I knew about myself or my actions I was trying to hold on to the rope. When I came to know any thing, I was not holding on to the rope, but was standing on the ground with my hands by my side. How long I had been there I could not say, because they deadened me to that extent that I did not know anything. I felt something pass from my neck way down to my extremities, like something when you hit your elbow. Said I, 'Gentlemen, I am dying, and I shall never see my friends nor family again.' They led me forward in the direction of the big road, and said, 'Now, old man, if you have any more arrangements to make, make them; your time is not long here. Are you not a Radical?' 'A Radical,' said I, as if I did not know what they meant. 'Yes,' said they, 'A Radical. How do you vote?' I told them. They said, 'If you have any arrangements to make, make them quick.' I said, 'I have nothing; if you are going to execute me, take me away from the house and suffer me to make a prayer.' They said, 'Go on.' I knelt down in the big road and tried to pray to my Maker for them, that peace might

come, and that these things might pass away. They stood
there with their six-shooters over my head. I supposed they
would kill me as scouts did men during the war, as I had
heard. I got through, and said 'Amen.' As I got up, they
fastened on to my arms again, and led me thirty or forty steps
back in the direction of the house. In the edge of the wood,
by the side of the big road, they halted me, and turned me
around square, front to the road. I saw the man with the
shrub come up again. I said, 'Gentlemen, how many are you
going to give me now?' They said, 'Make him pull off his
coat.' They commenced hitting me, and I commenced counting. I counted, 'One, two, three, four,' until they give me
six licks. It hurt desperately. I said 'Lord! have mercy on
me,' for I saw those people had no mercy, and there was no
one to apply to for relief but the Lord. They gave me the six
licks over my shoulders and across my back; they gave me
four, and I then said 'Ten.' The commander said 'Stop!
halt!' They then sent another person to whip me across the
legs, but how many licks he gave me I do not know. I reasonably suppose that first and last in the three whippings they
gave me that night, the very shortest was seventy-five licks."

His whole story will be found on pages 363 to 368 of Vol. 6,
of the *Reports.*

ABRAM COLBY (colored), fifty-two years old, member of Legislature from Greene Co., Ga., was taken out of his house at
night by 60 disguised men, and beaten with sticks and straps
until insensible and pronounced dead by one of the party.
Had not recovered one year afterwards. His little daughter
was so terrified that she died from the effects of her fright.
Had a small plantation, and was making a comfortable living.
Left home as soon afterwards as he could be moved. Went
home once after that, and the house was attacked and riddled
with bullets the first night after. Fled to Atlanta again.

The motive, as expresssly stated by themselves, was to prevent his taking part in politics as a Republican.

"They said to me 'Do you think you will ever vote another
damned Radical ticket?' I said, 'I will not tell you a lie.'
They said, 'No; do not lie to us.' I thought they would kill
me anyhow, and I might just as well tell the truth, so I said,
'If there was an election to-morrow, I would vote the Radical

ticket.' Then they set in and whipped me. I suppose they must have struck me a thousand licks in all, with sticks and straps. They left me for dead. I have been told that twenty-five of them whipped me after I was unconscious." [The object of this was that each one should be an actual *particeps criminis*, should there be any criminal proceedings in consequence of their action.]

This shows something of what it cost to be a Republican then, and yet Abram Colby was true and faithful to the party which gave him his liberty, even with his scarred and crippled body. The poor man counted it all only his part of the great sacrifice required to bring liberty and freedom to the enslaved.

He tells his story on pages 695 to 698, Vol. 7, of the *Reports*.

ALFRED RICHARDSON was a colored man of Clarke Co., Ga.; 34 years of age, and born a slave. He was a house-carpenter, and had a wife and three children. He was thrifty and industrious, and much looked up to by his own people. He was elected a member of the Legislature in 1868, was turned out the first session, but was reseated the next, and served out the term. The money he had saved at his trade he invested in the grocery business with his brother, who managed that, while he kept on with his carpentering. It seems unnecessary to say that he was a Republican.

One night, just before Christmas, 1870, he was aroused by a great outcry, and going into the streets to see what was the occasion of it, found a body of disguised men beating an old colored man to induce him to tell where Alfred Richardson was, and what defence he had made in anticipation of an attack from the Ku-Klux. The wife and children of the old man were screaming and hallooing for help, and begging the Ku-Klux not to beat the husband and father to death. They said he must go with them and show them where Alfred Richardson was, and get him to come ont. Of course, Alfred Richardson and the crowd of colored men with him ran when they found what was going on; and were fired at, some twenty or more shots lodging in the leg and hip of Alfred ·Richardson. The doctor fixed up his wounds, and in a few days he was able to travel about.

On the 18th of January an influential white man of the neighborhood came to him and said:

"There are some men about here that have something against you; and they intend to kill you or break you up. They say you are making too much money; that they do not allow any nigger to rise that way; and they intend to break you up, and then they can rule the balance of the niggers when they get you off." He said, "They wanted me to join their party, but I told them I did not want to do it; I never knew you to do any wrong, and these are a parcel of low-down men, and I don't want to join any such business, but I tell you, you had better keep your eyes open, for they are after you."

The poor colored man, in reply, asked what he had done that he should thus be driven away from his home and the property he had accumulated by his honesty and thrift. He had always been instrumental in keeping the peace between the colored and white people, and when outbreaks had occurred he was the only one who could influence his people and bring them to their senses. He talked with other white people, those who had employed him at different times, and they told him not to run away, that it was but idle talk to frighten him.

That same night they came in fantastic disguise and tried to break open the door of this poor colored man's cabin. The door had been barred very securely, in anticipation of this visit, with long staples at the side and scantling bars across it. Though eight or ten of them ran together against the door to burst it open, they could not do it. One had a new patent ax, and with it succeeded in cutting down the door.

But let Richardson tell the rest of the story in his own words:—

"I stood and looked at him until he had cut it spang through; then I thought I had better go upstairs; I did so. I thought I would stand at the head of the stair-steps and shoot them as they came up; but they broke in the lower door and came up stairs firing in every direction. I could not stand in the stairway to shoot at them. I had some small arms back in the garret. There was a door up there about large enough for one man to creep in. I thought I had better go in there and maybe they would not find me—probably they would miss me and I could make my escape. They all came upstairs. My wife opened the window to call out for help, and a fellow shot at her some twelve or fourteen shots through that window while she was hallooing. A whole crowd came up, and when they saw that window open they said, 'He has jumped out of the window,' and they hallooed to the fellows on the ground to shoot on top of the house. Thinking I had gone through the window they all went downstairs except one man. He went and looked in the cuddy-hole where I was, and saw me there; he hallooed to the rest of the fellows that he had found me; but they had got downstairs and some of them were on the piazza. Then he commenced firing and shot me three times. He lodged two balls in my side and one in the right arm. That weakened me pretty smartly. After he had shot his loads all out he said to the rest of them, 'Come back up here; I have got him, and I have shot him but he is not quite dead; come up and let's finish him.' I crept from the door of the little room where I was to the stairway. They came up-stairs with their pistols in their hands and a man behind with a light. I shot one of them as he got on the top step; they gathered him up by the legs, and then they all ran and left me. I never saw any more of them that night, and I have not seen them since. I have heard talk of them, and they say they will have me, no matter where I go."

The remainder of this interesting story may be found on pages 1 to 19 of Vol. 6, of the *Reports.*

THOMAS M. ALLEN was a colored man and a Baptist clergy-man of Jasper County, Georgia. He was not a pure African, but was one of those frequent combinations of son and servant of the whites which abounded under the slave régime. His mother was at once the servant of her master and the mother of his children. They lived in the city of Charleston, and during the life of the paternal master their lot was not a hard one. The master was fond of luxury; the slave-girl was not only faithful but beautiful, and she and her children were much indulged. There came a time, too, when the conscience of the lordly planter smote him for the wrong he had inflicted on his paramour and his own flesh and blood. The pains of death got hold upon him and he made his will, giving freedom to "the girl Jennie" and to the two children which she had

borne to him.  He also devoted to the maintenance of the trio,
and the proper education and tuition of his son and daughter,
the sum of ten thousand dollars.  No doubt he felt better for
this act of tardy justice, and it is devoutly to be hoped that
his kind intent "was accounted unto him for righteousness,"
and that his death-bed was more peaceful for having performed it.

It was, however, of little avail to the dusky handmaiden or
her innocent children.  Hardly had the breath left the body of
the master-husband, and before his body had been committed
to the tomb, they were in the hands of the slave-driver, and
the executors of the will could find no beneficiaries to receive
the bequest.  So, at least, they reported to the proper court;
the legacy was declared to have lapsed, and it was not until
"freedom" came that Thomas Allen knew that such a legacy
had been bequeathed to him.  It was then too late to obtain
any advantage thereby, for thirty odd years of slavery, harsh
and grim, lay between the day of discovery and the death of
the devisor.

This slave-life had been hard but not altogether unprofitable
to him.  He had been allowed to hire his time, and had been
accustomed to practice thrift and self-denial.  He had stolen a
few grains of knowledge, also, and learned to read his Bible
with some difficulty and to write a reasonably fair hand, despite the laws which forbade the tree of knowledge to the
slave.  When, however, the day of freedom came he found
himself only with wife and children about him and nothing to
show for his labor any more than the rest of his unfortunate
race.  He was not disheartened, but at once went to work to
make up the loss of his best years, and when Reconstruction
opened the way to the exercise of political power by his race,
he was chosen by them to represent the county in the Legislature.  Already by his industry he had acquired what was
among his people accounted a nice little sum.  He had a substantial double log-house, a horse or two, some stock, and a
good little plantation, which he cultivated with his family,
and in those years of high prices had made very profitable,

He was one of those colored men who were unseated in the first Legislature of his State by unlawful and fraudulent means, and was afterwards restored to his place in that body. It was in the fall of 1868 that he was unseated upon a fraudulent pretext, which it is unnecessary here to consider. On the 16th of October, 1868, it came his turn to learn by practical demonstration that only the forms of freedom were for the colored man. Its rights, privileges, and valuable facts and franchises were still reserved to the master-race. How he learned that lesson let him tell:—

"Just before that, October 16th, 1868, I was at home and two white men came to the field where I was working. I heard them speaking to my children and asking for their father. I came up over the hill, and they told me that the Radicals had expelled me from the Legislature, and that I ought to take with the Democrats now, and take the stump for Seymour and Blair. I said I did not consider that I was expelled by the Radical party. They were friends; Mr. Phelps was one, and he said that I could do more good by preaching the Gospel and leaving political affairs alone. Then they went off.

"I called a political meeting in town to organize a Grant club, or Grant Rangers as we called it. Senator Wallace, who was expelled at the same time, was to come there and help out this meeting. We were to have the meeting on the 17th, but Mr. Wallace did not come to my house until the 18th. Captain Bartlett told some colored people a day or two before the meeting that they had better stay away from town; that he did not think I would live to see the meeting. Captain Bartlett is a lawyer there.

"On the 16th or 17th I went home; I felt very bad; I felt very curious. The man running the place there said that if any one came there at any time of night not to open the door. I went home, and drove my hogs up and put them in the pen, and when they brought in the cotton I weighed it. I felt so strangely that I went into a log cabin and ate my supper, and went back into the house and got a Testament and read a chapter, and went to bed very early.

"About 2 o'clock my wife woke me up and said there were persons all around the house; that they had been there for half an hour, and were calling for me. I heard them call again, and I asked them what they wanted and who they were. One said, 'Andy Minter,' who was a friend of mine. My wife said that was not his voice. I asked what they wanted. They said they wanted a light; that they had been hunting and the dogs had treed something, and they wanted a light. I tried to find something to make a light, but could not. They said, 'Have you no matches?' I said, 'No.' I had some, but I forgot that I had any. They asked me to come out. At this time my brother-in-law waked up and said, 'Who are they, Thomas?' I said I did not know; one said that he is Andy Minter, but it is not. He said, 'I will get up and give them a light.' I said, 'You had better not.' I stepped to the side window and opened it and looked out, and said, 'Emanuel will give you a light.' My wife told me to come away and shut the window. I went back to my room and went to bed.

"Emanuel made a big light in his part of the house. It was a frame house, but the partition that separated my part from his did not go clear up to the roof, and I could see the light. He put on his shoes and vest and hat; that was all he was found with after he was killed. He opened the door and hollered, 'Who are you?' He hollered twice, and then two guns were fired. He seemed to fall, and I and my wife hollered and his wife hollered. I jumped up and ran back to the fireplace, where I started to get a light, and then started to go over the partition to him. I threw a clock down, and then I thought of the closet there and went through it to him, and my wife closed the door. I hollered for Joe, a third man on the place, to come up and bring his gun, for Emanuel was killed. He did not come for some time, and then I was so excited that I could not recognize his voice. After a time I let him in. We made up a light, and then I saw my brother-in-law lying on his back as he fell. I examined him : there were four or five number-one buck-shot in his breast. He seemed to be dying very fast. Joe said, 'What shall we do?' I said, 'Go for Dr. Walker.' I just had on my shirt and drawers, and was bareheaded; my boots and everything else were in my room. My wife was looking over into the room. I asked for my shoes, but she would not give them to me; she said I would be killed if I went out. I examined him again. He had on copperas pants, and near the waist-band a slug had gone through. While we were examining him he died.

"Next morning, as soon as it was light, I went out and counted one hundred and eighty shots in the house, and they will be there until Judgment, or until the house shall rot down. The white men who came there the next day and held an inquest over him decided that three guns had been fired, one loaded with slugs, one with buck-shot, and one with small shot. Two of the shot went into the beadstead where his wife and children were in bed.  He laid there until we could get a crowd of white men to hold an inquest over him.

"By this time Mr. Wallace arrived.  He got there about 10 o'clock in the day.  When Mr. Wallace drove up to the gate these white men who were holding the inquest were sitting under a tree inside of the gate.  He said, "Allen, you have had a death out here.'  I said, 'Yes.'  He said, 'Why did you not kill some of those fellows ?'  I said, 'There was not a gun in the house, and if there had been I could not see anybody.'  He said, 'We do not allow men to come to Milledgeville and do such things.'  The white men seemed to be excited about it.  I took him right into my house, and he took his pistol from under the cushions of his buggy, a bottle of liquor from under the seat, and his carpet-bag, and carried them into my room.  Colonel James Wilson came in and said, 'By God, Allen, I told you six months ago that we would not submit to negroism in this State; did I not tell you they would kill you ?'  I said, 'Yes, but I did not believe it; I did not think any body had any thing against me; I preached for you all during the war, when you could not get a white preacher, for all had gone into the army ; I did not think any body would kill me for my political sentiment.'  He said, 'I told you they would do it; you leave the country now or they will murder you and your wife and children.'  Mr. Wallace, who had not said any thing, then said, 'If I was Allen, I would not do it.  If I was him, I would get half a dozen guns and some friends, and guard the house and kill the first man that comes up.'  Wilson then turned to him and said, 'By God, who are you ?'  He said, 'I am Mr. Johnson;' he changed his name.  Wilson said, 'You had better keep still; for if these men hear you, they will kill you.'  Wallace said, 'There is no danger of death.'  They got through the inquest that evening."

It will be seen that Mr. Wallace was taught a lesson of prudence by the chivalrous coroner.  The story should stop here, but there are two or three other facts narrated by this witness which are peculiarly interesting.  Colonel James Wilson was the coroner of the county.  The usual idea of the Southern gentleman is that he is generous, kindly, and brave, above all pettiness, and only subject to the human infirmities of arrogance and passion.  Note the conduct of the gallant colonel in the following extract from Allen's testimony :—

"Wilson came to me about sundown and said, 'I am going to have that body buried, coffin or no coffin; I am going to have my fee, and I can not get it without its being buried.' I said, 'You can not bury it without a coffin ; he has left some bales of cotton, and you hold on until the coffin comes.' He said, 'Will you be responsible ?' I said, 'Yes,' and then he went off. That night some of the parties staid up there and we organized what we called the Grant Rangers, while the body lay there in the next room. Sunday morning I had my son catch my horse and I came on here to Atlanta."

The effect of this and numerous other like exploits of the Klan upon the political complexion of the county is very clearly perceivable from the following :—

"We did not poll but three votes in that county for General Grant, out of nine hundred and odd votes which we had. There were nine hundred and sixty colored voters, and about six hundred white voters. There were three votes polled for General Grant, two by colored men and one by a white man."

The reason of this is perhaps made even clearer by the notice received by Allen on the morning of election-day. It ran as follows :—

" *To Thomas Allen, (Freedman).*

"Tom, you are in great danger ; you are going heedless with the radicals against the interest of the conservative white population, and I tell you if you do not change your course before the election for the ratification of the infernal constitution your days are numbered, and they will be but few. Just vote or use your influence for the radicals, or for the constitution, and you go up certain. My advice to you, Tom, is to stay at home if you value your life, and not vote at all and advise all of your race to do the same thing. You are marked and closely watched by K. K. K. (or in plain words Ku-Klux). Take heed ; a word to the wise is sufficient.
" By order of GRAND CYCLOPS."

This story is told by THOMAS M. ALLEN, free man of color, beginning on page 607 of Vol. 7 of the *Reports.*

### HENRY LOWTHER.

The whole story of Henry Lowther, of Wilkinson County, Ga., because of its peculiar character, can not be transcribed into these pages. And yet it is a most instructive one, which no man should fail to con with some care, who desires to realize the differences between the Northern and Southern "civilizations." It has seemed incredible to many that men of good character, refined and Christian people, should be guilty of such seeming barbarity. In this case it will be seen how coolly the Southern man regards suffering when inflicted as punishment or torture upon one proscribed by the prejudice of race or under the ban of society for adverse opinions. The barbarity of the Indian at his worst estate is mercy compared with its unpitying coldness. It is neither savagery nor hate. There is nothing of the rush and intensity of anger about it. It is simply that cold, unmoved, immovable inertness of heart which men seldom acquire, even toward the inanimate creation, except by frequent observance of their sufferings. It is the most terrible inheritance which Slavery left to its votaries. It reminds one strangely of that culminating curse which fell upon him who held Israel in bondage, of which we are told that "God *hardened* Pharaoh's heart." It is the peculiar and characteristic bane of Slavery. They who are afflicted *with* it are as deserving of our pity as they who suffer *by* it. Yet it is one of the facts which underlie and account for all that has been narrated, and however horrible and loathsome some of its manifestations may be, they are not on that account to be passed over or disregarded.

Henry Lowther was an industrious, prosperous colored man—a Republican of influence and prominence. He refused to work for men who did not pay him, and from his skill and business sagacity had acquired some considerable estate. He was just turned of forty, and had been many times threatened by the Ku-Klux, and his house once broken open, when he was accused of having formed a conspiracy with certain of his own color to waylay and resist the Klan on their midnight raids. Upon such a sham charge of conspiracy he was arrested and thrown into jail. He was taken out of the jail one night in the Fall, and with no clothing but his shirt was taken to a swamp near by and there maltreated in a manner too horrible to relate —which reminds one of the vengeance of the Comanche or the religious hate of ancient heathen tyrants. We give a few lines only from his testimony to illustrate what has been said. After he had suffered agonies worse than death in the swamp, they turned him loose, and, nearly naked, faint from loss of blood, he staggered back towards town.  He says:—

"The first man's house I got to was the jailer's.  I called him up and asked him to go to the house and get my clothes. He said he could not go ; I said, 'You *must ;* I am naked and nearly frozen to death.'  That was about three o'clock in the night.  He had a light in the house, and there was a party of men standing in the door.  I told him I wanted him to come out and give me some attention.  He said he could not come. I could hardly walk then.  I went on about ten steps further and I met the jailer's son-in-law.  I asked him to go and get my clothes; and he said 'No,' and told me to go and lie down. I went right on and got up to a store; there were a great many men sitting along on the store piazza.  I knew some of them, but I did not look at them much.  They asked me what I wanted; I said I wanted a doctor.  They told me to go on and lie down.  I had then to stop and hold on to the side of the house to keep from falling.  I staid there a few minutes and then went on to a doctor's house, about a quarter of a mile, and called him aloud twice.  He did not answer me.  The next thing I knew I was lying on the sidewalk in the street— seemed to have just waked up out of sleep.  I thought to my- self, 'Did I lie down and go to sleep ?'  I wanted some water; I had to go about a quarter of a mile to get some water.  I was getting out of breath, but the water helped me considerably. I went to a house about fifty yards further; I called to a col- ored woman to wake my wife up; she was in town.  I hap- pened to find my son there, and he went back for the doctor. When he got there, the doctor answered the first time he called him.  The reason he did not answer me was that he was off on this raid.  I asked the doctor where he was when I was at his house, and he said he was asleep.  I said, 'I was at your house.' The men kept coming in and saying to me that I did not get to the doctor's house, and I said I did.  After two or three times I took the hint, and said nothing more about that.  But I told my son the next morning to go there and see if there was not a large puddle of blood at the gate.  They would not let him go.  But some colored women came to see me and told me that the blood was all over town—at the doctor's gate and everywhere else.  I was running a stream all the time I was trying to find the doctor, and I thought I would bleed to death."  (Pages 356 to 363, Vol. 6, *Reports.*)

Here we close the chapter.  We have spared the reader far more terrible relations than the foregoing, because we did not set out to make him "sup full of horrors," and have therefore only re-cited enough to indicate the broader range of facts.  Even were we disposed to enlarge the record, we should be compelled to desist out of respect for morality and good taste, many of the recitals being too horrible and indecent to repeat in print. Much less fiendish and devoid of originality were the thumb-screws and racks and boiling oil of the Spanish Inquisition, or the terrors of the stake to which the wild Indian was wont to consign his captives.

Every one of these dreadful tales points unerringly to the same significant facts, that the victims were either colored men or the friends of the colored race, and their rank offense con-sisted in trying to realize the "freedom" which the Nation gave to the slave—but has not been able to secure to him.

## CHAPTER XI.

### SOUTHERN SENTIMENT.

INTOLERANCE has always been the distinguishing characteristic of Southern thought.   Even in the *ante-bellum* days, the
conflict of parties was much fiercer at the South than at the
North.   The fact that less than one-third of the population
controlled, absolutely, the action and conduct of the other
two-thirds—the negroes and poor whites—made laws in their
own interest, and for the suppression of all independence and
individuality on the part of the others, and were, in short, the
self-appointed rulers of the land, no doubt in great measure
accounted for this peculiarity.   The sort of feudalism which
existed at the South, in connection with that sense of isolation
which must always prevail where the land is held in immense
tracts, and the laborers are either slaves or dependents, no
doubt did much to encourage that pride of opinion which en-
abled them to arrogate to themselves the distinction of being
"the Southern People" to the exclusion of an equal number of
poor white renters, croppers, and mechanics, as well as a like
number of slaves and free negroes.                                    44

This exclusion, which is a thing almost incredible to the
Northern mind, was all the more easily accomplished by means
of the inherent differences between the forms of government
which formerly prevailed at the South and those obtaining at
the North.   We have been accustomed to consider these differences as all embraced in the one institution of Slavery, and
it is undeniable that they were so closely interwoven with that
institution, and became so considerable an element in its per-
petuity and prosperity, that it is perhaps impossible entirely to
separate their effects and to trace the growth and development
of each.   There is, however, no doubt that a careful analysis
of the respective forms of government prevailing in the two

sections, irrespective of the fact of Slavery, will show the most radical differences even as far back as the old Colonial times.

The strong individualism which marked the Northern colonists, and which was ever at war with that Puritanism which was its own parent, was almost entirely lacking in the Southern colonies. The bulk of the land in these was absorbed by vast holdings, and the larger portion of the laboring classes consisted of those who had been gathered from the peasant classes of the Old World, and induced to emigrate only to hold the same relations toward the lordly proprietors in the New; or else they were the imported refuse of the prisons and alms-houses of England. The commonalty of the North, whether of English or Dutch extraction, came hither of their own free will and accord from the Old World, either to escape oppression which weighed heavily upon them there, or to lift themselves above the stations which they had previously occupied. They were the best, bravest and most enterprising of their respective classes—those who rebelled at untoward fortune, and determined to improve their fate by the exercise of energy, thrift, and fortitude in the western wilds. The laborers of the South were either ignorant and mercenary *emigrés*, who were seduced by the promise of greater wages put forth by the proprietors, or those unfortunates who chose exile rather than starvation or transportation, rather than the prison or the gallows; for it must be remembered that in those days the theft of a few shillings was a capital offense. To put it in a word, the colonists of the North came impelled by the spur of their own conviction; those of the South came on account of extraneous persuasion or compulsion. The former *came;* the latter *were brought.*

This difference is clearly perceptible in the governments which were organized after the Revolution, and which became component parts of the Union. In the one section the rights of the many were most carefully guarded; in the other the rights and privileges of the few were accorded the special protection. The *township system*, that perfect crystallization of the primeval democratic idea, with its open town-meeting and untrammeled discussion of all matters, both great and small, affecting the interest of the municipality, became, as it were, the unit around which the States of the North were builded. All the institutions which grew out of it were calculated to encourage individuality and personal independence. The North became, therefore, emphatically a nation of freemen and equals. Public education flourished as a part of the statal economy, and the idea came universally to prevail that the government was indeed " of the people, by the people, and for the people." Suffrage soon became almost unrestricted; no qualification beyond that of citizenship was required to make one eligible to any official position; almost all officers were elective by the body of the people; labor was accounted reputable, and the successful farmer or mechanic found no obstacle in the way of his social or political aspiration; and the humblest pupil of the town-meeting found every door yielding readily to his industry and perseverance, until even the bronze gates of the Capitol opened to receive him as a national lawmaker.

At the South all this was reversed. The county was the lowest automatic governmental unit. Authority flowed from the center toward the circumference. The great body of the officers were appointed instead of being elective. The judiciary, the magistracy, the financial officers of the counties, in almost all these States, were selected by the Executive or by the dominant party in the Legislature. There were no smaller municipal subdivisions than the county. There was no such *witenagemote* as the town-meeting, in which the poorest and humblest might have his unrestricted say—might advocate his own theory as to the public weal. Suffrage was restricted in most States to the land-owner; only the possessor of an estate of freehold was eligible to official position, to the magistracy, or to service upon the grand and petit juries; the opening of a public road, the building of a bridge, or any matter of purely local interest, no matter how trivial, could be determined upon only by the County Court or some similar tribunal. There was no subdivision of the commonwealth into self-regulating municipalities where the suffragan acted for himself without the intervention of a representative. As a consequence, the people grew accustomed to being governed instead of governing themselves. Democratic progress was so slow that the impatient student of its past is apt to deny that any was made. Popular education never obtained a firm foothold there as a part of the governmental machinery. As a result, the masses were ignorant and poor; the few, arrogant and rich. The results are well epitomized in Massachusetts and North Carolina. In the former, slavery was abolished by the growth and eradicating force of individual liberty; in the latter it was only uprooted as a result of war. In the former, less than four in every hundred of its native white adult citizens are unable to read and write; in the latter, there are twenty-eight out of every hundred of the native *whites* who cannot read the ballots which they cast. In the former, the average wealth *per capita* is twelve hundred and fifty dollars; in the latter, it is three hundred dollars.

46

With these governmental differences came also Slavery, and added its blighting power to the disabilities which weighed upon the already handicapped masses of the South. The slaveholder was also the squirarch and the legislator. Materially, morally, politically and intellectually, the laborer was the dependent and follower of the landlord. Thus it resulted that a minority ruled the South and arrogated to itself the rights, privileges and importance of the whole. The few snubbed and suppressed the many. "The South" came to mean only this dominant minority. Upon all subjects touching their own privileges, this minority—the oligarchy of the South—was practically unanimous. Against anything which tended to lessen their power they stood as one man. Against free suffrage and public education they fought long and fiercely. Against free-labor, free-thought and free-speech they stood as a wall of fire which none might overleap. Behind this bulwark, Slavery grew strong, malignant, and intolerant of opposition or difference.

This same people, ignorant and hostile, or arrogant and intolerant, exasperated by defeat and humiliated by poverty, hating the North as an ancient enemy and its institutions as the source of social, moral and political corruption and degeneracy, constitute the South of to-day. The ruling class is as arrogant, the poor as abject as ever; for there has been nothing to change their relations or characteristics for the better. To these attributes are added the exasperation and humiliation resulting from the enfranchisement and political exaltation of the negro. To the former master this seemed an insult ; to the poor white a threat. To the former it meant a loss of his possessions ; to the latter the political co-ordination of his sole inferior.

From such mental and political conditions came that intolerance which the Northern mind finds it so hard to understand. It was in a soil thus prepared that Ku-Kluxism struck its roots wide and deep, flourishing as no exotic could, with the strong, vigorous growth of an indigenous stock. The following extracts from the reports will give some faint idea of the character and intensity of this feeling.

It is very tersely described by Mr. JOHN C. NORRIS, of Warren County, Georgia. He had been elected Sheriff, and states that—

"The newspaper in my town gave notice that any one who went on my bond would be considered a Radical and denounced as such in every way." In explanation of this, he adds :—"To call a man a Radical, in that country, is worse than to call him a horse-thief. . . . A man who is called a Radical is not considered as having any character at all." (Vol. 6: p. 194.)

Volumes could not express the feeling more clearly, and thousands can to-day sadly testify of its truth.

This sentiment was echoed with varying degrees of intensity of expression by nearly every Republican who was examined by the committee. It is especially well put by Hon. JAMES ATKINS, a very moderate and thoughtful native Republican, who was appointed Collector of Internal Revenue in Georgia by President Johnson. He says :—

"I think they (the dominant Southern whites) look at everything very much in the light of their old prejudices and the feelings growing out of the war. . . . It (the feeling of hostility and intolerance) operates on our church relations, our social relations, in fact in all the relations of life. . . . I do not know *a single instance of a feeling of warm personal friendship between persons of different politics!"* (Vol. 6: p. 522.)

The same witness explains the Southern sense of the term " carpet-bagger" : —

" It has become very much in vogue to call any man a ' carpet-bagger ' who came here from the North. Judge Polk, who has lived here for *forty years*, is called a ' carpet-bagger.' I can name a dozen men who have lived here and raised up families, who are yet called ' carpet-baggers.' A citizen of a Northern State coming here and identifying himself with our interests would not have an equal chance for success and happiness unless he ignored politics, took no side, or was on the Democratic side." (Vol. 6: p. 526.)

He further illustrates the condition of the Northern man at the South, and shows how he is not even allowed to remain neutral upon political questions :—

" It is very hard," he says, " for a man simply to hold his own views and nothing more. He is pressed for a statement of his views, to be outspoken, and whenever he does that they ban him, leave him alone; there is no question about that. I have known men who came here and for a while kept themselves quiet, and then declared their political sentiments, and the feeling toward them changed at once." (Vol. 6: p. 526.)

JOSIAH SHERMAN, a Vermont mechanic, who undertook to cultivate cotton and " conciliation " in Georgia, gives this as the upshot of his experience and observation:—

" The idea in my section is that a Northern man has no rights here which need be respected." And again:—" A Northern man has no business to start in trade or any kind of business here, expecting a fair show." (Vol. 7: p. 1151.)

The following from the testimony of Hon. A. R. WRIGHT, of Georgia, ex-judge and ex-Congressman, and one of the most open defenders of the Ku-Klux, speaks volumes of unintended truth:—

" It cost a man nothing to be a Union man in the North;

but in the South a Union man, besides being ostracized and de-   47
spised, carried his life in his hand." (Vol. 6: p. 118.)

Such feeling does not die out in an hour, and helps to
explain the animosity which is felt towards those who acted
with this despised class.

In this connection it may be well to quote one pithy
passage from an article in the *International Review* of February, 1880, reviewing the course of Reconstruction in South
Carolina, by Mr. EDWARD HOGAN, himself an admitted ad-
mirer and champion of Gov. Wade Hampton. He says:   48

"It was practically social ostracism for the South Carolinian to withhold his sympathy from the Ku-Klux of the early
days, and from the Rifle Clubs after the 'Mississippi Campaign.' . . . There was no room in South Carolina for a Republican who tried to keep out of politics." And again, he says:
" Southern families visit each other, and occasionally Northern
people are invited to social gatherings; but not so freely as to
prevent an appearance of dislike. Republican office holders
and politicians are debarred Southern society; and the South
Carolinian who becomes a Republican meets with less consideration than would be accorded to a dog from the families of
Democrats. Republican physicians can get no practice except
among negroes. Republican lawyers say that a man, in order
not to prejudice his case in the courts, must employ Democratic
counsel, though his inclinations may be otherwise. . . .
" A man cannot run a cotton mill in South Carolina on Republican principles."

Another illustration of this feeling is the almost utter
absence of young Republicans in the South. Very few are to
be found in any section under thirty-five years of age or who
were not married at the close of the war or soon thereafter.
The tenor of social life is such as to preclude their having
pleasant relations with their young associates and contracting
reasonable marriages in their own circle without abjuring, as a
rule, their Republican principles.

"What," cried a Democratic orator upon the hustings in
North Carolina, "What has my opponent done that everybody
might not do as well?" "What have I done?" was the quick
and pungent retort, uttered with conscious pride in the

strength of character it attested, "*I have married a Democrat's daughter without turning Democrat !*" It was enough.

In all that has been said and written upon this subject there has been nothing more clearly showing forth the relations of the northern man at the South to those by whom he was surrounded, than the following extract from a pamphlet published by Hon. HENRY C. DIBBLE, of New Orleans, in 1877:—

"The greater portion of the Northern men in these States, who have been classed and branded as carpet-baggers, were living in the South when the Reconstruction acts were passed. There is a popular belief that most of them were attracted to the Southern States by the hope and prospect of gaining offices through the votes of the newly enfranchised blacks. That some of them who were there at the time in the public service remained only to obtain political preferment, and that there were political vultures there, as elsewhere, is true. But the larger number of the class were men who had remained in the South upon leaving the army, at the close of the war. At that time the Reconstruction measures had not been proposed. So soon after the triumph of our armies, it was not generally deemed a very grave offense for Northern men to settle in the South. They might even entertain and proclaim the political sentiments and ideas which they brought with them, as the men did who moved westward to build up Iowa, Kansas, and Nebraska. The new doctrine, that the citizen who does not conform his political sentiments to his surroundings shall be deemed an alien, had not yet been announced. Many of them were young men who had married wives in their new homes; others brought their families with them, or were unmarried. They were lawyers, ministers, doctors, merchants, speculators, farmers, teachers, editors, or clerks, who had left the army to remain, or who had come here in the service of the Freedman's Bureau. Many of them were poor, hoping to make fortunes; others were rich, and thought to increase their store fourfold and fivefold from the great productive wealth of the rich soil. Born amid the rigors of the North, they were enamored of the glorious sunny sky and the most genial climate on the face of the earth. Many of them were noble, honorable and true men. Many of them were not, which will be found true of any other class in this or any other part of the country. That so many of them became active politicians may be ascribed to several causes. The greater number of them were just out of the army, with restless minds and impulses readily quickened by the same influences which aroused and concentrated the members of the dominant party in Congress. Men who go out to fight for political views continue to have an interest in civil life in the ascendency of those views. Then the returned Confederates, after they had gained control of their States in 1865, under President Johnson's Reconstruction policy, began to manifest considerable bitterness towards Northern men living there, until at times and places it became unbearable. This bitterness was displayed in business and social ostracism; it was doubtless traceable, in a degree at least, to the influences of caste prejudice. Northern men would sometimes presume to befriend a negro in a contest with a white man, and they at once lost social caste. All this was natural enough; there is no use to carp. It is well, however, to endeavor to trace these observed results to their natural causes. The term carpet-bagger was applied to all Northern men who came South during or since the war, and who actively participated in politics with the Republicans. The epithet was intended to suggest the belief that such persons were here to remain only while they held office. It mattered not if they were men of property, and above reproach. All were carpet-baggers who came from the North, and who were openly and actively Republicans. There were active Democratic politicians in the South who were new-comers from other States, and who gained office, and who had no other means of support. They were not carpet-baggers, however, because they had not lost caste by political association with the negroes.

"Altogether, the white Republicans comprised a mere fraction of the white population of the South, probably not more than ten per cent of the whole. Their number varied in the different States and localities in accordance with local influences.

"During the period of Reconstruction, the white Republicans of both classes were almost universally ostracized in society, and to a great extent in business, by the Southern whites. I use the term Southern whites for convenience, to designate all of our race in the South who were not Republicans. The ostracism by society of all carpet-baggers, without regard to their moral or social worth, was carried to the most painful extremity. It was visited upon their children, on the streets and in the schools, and upon their wives in all places—many of them noble women, who were publicly and privately scorned and hated by those among whom they had been born, or in whose midst they had found homes with their husbands. The Southern Republicans were not so entirely cut off from their associations, only because they had family ties, which tended somewhat to neutralize the hatred. To denounce a carpet-bagger or scallawag (a name given to Southern Republicans) as infamous, was proper at all times. In the large centers, like New Orleans, the white Republicans were not without pleasant society, but they found it alone in interassociation. In the frequent attacks made upon Republicans, by the press and by individuals, there was more open violence displayed towards carpet-baggers than towards Southern Republicans. Carpet-baggers were more hated, because, added to their being political associates of negroes, and therefore degraded, they were also Yankees, whom it was traditional to hate. And then Southern Republicans, in many instances, were able to maintain a certain restraint upon their enemies by accepting at all times the duello. The carpet-bagger, as a class, educated in the North to despise this custom, refused to acknowledge it, and only resorted to arms when actually attacked. They enjoyed, however, comparative immunity from personal assaults; they were always armed, and ready enough to fight when attacked. The ostracism of Republicans in business became a tenet of the Democratic party in the South. It was proclaimed in the political canvass, and individual Democrats were not infrequently denounced for giving patronage to Radicals, and for associating in public places with Republican leaders. To the Northern man, this ostracism on account of political affiliation seems not only absurd, but reprehensible in the greatest degree. The Southerners did not lack the intelligence to see that it could not be justified, consequently they either denied it as a fact, or offered a false explanation. 'These Republicans,' said they, 'are all infamous—guilty of all the crimes in the calendar, and therefore not fit associates of gentlemen.' Yes! They were guilty of the greatest social offense known in these slave-holding communities; they had affiliated with negroes—had fallen into the caste of Pariahs."

Mr. DIBBLE, in this very valuable pamphlet, offers the best explanation of this feeling that has ever been attempted. He says:—

"In order that we may comprehend the disposition of the Southerners towards the blacks, let me use an illustration: Men do not hate dogs; on the contrary, there exists a strong friendship between master and brute. But if a dog attempts to get upon a man's table, and persists in his objectionable course, he is apt to be shot for his trouble, and we approve the killing. The Southerners did not hate the negroes; on the contrary, there existed between the old slave-holding class and the blacks very kindly relations—far more so than existed between the races in the North. But the average Southerner looked upon the blacks at all times and in all respects as inferior beings. They were entitled to be treated kindly, and to be protected in their sphere; but they must not attempt to pass beyond it. Taught by the laws of caste to look upon himself and his class as alone entitled to exercise the prerogatives of citizenship, he resented the disposition of the black man to claim his franchise about in the same spirit in which a man will shoot a dog which has climbed upon the table and will not down."

Mr. HOGAN, in the *International Review* for February, 1880, justly measures the force of this feeling when he says:—

"If the negro in the future votes the Democratic ticket he will be safe. . . . If he persists in still being a Republican, and boldly calling himself a citizen, no amount of peaceful professions or kindly consideration will save him from being pushed aside by men who indignantly deny him to be their political equal. A leader among the extreme Democrats of the State, General Martin Gary, typifies this latent sentiment of hostility to the negro in the following words: 'The North does not know what it asks of us. No laws or regulations can overcome instinct allied to public opinion. God never made the two races to unite on *any* ground of equality, and they never will. The white man is the negro's superior, and as such he must remain. The negro cannot be made my social *or political* equal by any of your laws, and I will never acknowledge him as such!'"

50

It is, of course, useless to call particular attention to the hundreds of witnesses who refer to this feeling, since but few do so with any discrimination as to its cause. The fact of its existence is declared or assumed by all except a few who shield themselves behind a general denial of ill-feeling toward the race. In the sense in which the words are used these statements are true; in the sense in which they are read at the North they are false, and, in not a few instances, were intended to deceive. Still further information may be obtained on this subject by carefully studying some of the experiences narrated in another chapter. It is this feeling which is at the bottom of all the Southern hostility to white Republicans.

The Southern view of the colored man and his relations as a political factor seem to be more difficult for the Northern mind to apprehend than any other feature of the Reconstruction era. And yet they are perfectly simple and easy to be understood if we will but keep in mind one single proposition. The Southern man—and in this case we use the term as including all Southern whites—has no antipathy to the negro *as such*—that is to the negro as something less than a man—or at least less than a white man. Regarding him as human only as he is sufficiently intelligent to do a portion of man's work, but without any of the inherent rights or ruling attributes which mark other races of the *genus homo*, as less than man and more than brute, and thereby fitted by nature to serve the higher race and subserve all a master's wants, they have in general only kindly feelings for him. It is a mistake, too, to suppose that this feeling is an incident of ownership. The fact of emancipation has not at all changed the Southern man's conception of the negro's place in nature, or of the proper relation between him and the Caucasian. The legal relation of slavery he admits to be ended, but the natural relation is not affected thereby in the least. The freedman is no less an inferior, no more a man, to his apprehension, than was the slave.

So the mere fact of emancipation would not have stirred up any great hostility against the blacks if they had still remained in some inferior and servile relation, subject to the government direction and control of the whites, their old masters. It was the attempt to make them political equals of the whites which exasperated the latter, because of an implied degradation by being put on the same plane with natural inferiors. This sentiment, so natural to a Southern man, is almost inexplicable to the Northerner, who feels no degradation in acknowledging the *political* equality of any and all men, even those whom he knows to be his social and intellectual inferiors. It not unfrequently requires years of actual experience, in the midst of this sentiment, to understand its intensity and universality. It is for this reason, chiefly, that the Northern tourist or transitory reporter becomes, in almost every case, the most delusive exponent of the state of feeling at the South. He interprets

the Southern man's language according to the formulas of his
Northern lexicon. When the Southern man says that he has
the kindest feeling to the negro, *in his place*, he means in the
place for which, according to the Southerner's notions, nature
designed him. His Northern listener thinks he means simply
a laborer or hired servant, and is struck with his justice, lib-
erality, and reasonableness. When the old master says that
he is willing that the negro should have all his rights, his
simple-hearted Northern listener thinks he means the right to
exercise all his political privileges. Not at all. He only means
that he should have the wages he earns, and be protected in
person and property. This he is willing to accord him as a
fair thing, which the white race are bound in honor to secure
him, so long as he does not interfere with *their* privileges and
seek to share the governing and controlling power. As a mere
servitor, he regards the negro kindly; as a political integer,
he looks upon him with unappeasable hostility.

Judge AUGUSTUS R. WRIGHT, of Georgia, heretofore alluded
to as a vigorous and bold apologist for the Klan, gives a hint
of this feeling when he says:—

" We are very much dissatisfied with that part of the constitution [universal suffrage]. I wish I could put a hundred thousand negro voters in Massachusetts and let them feel it as we
do. If it was meant as a punishment for rebellion, all right;
only it is a strange sort of punishment—a new grade. The old
rule of the law was to hang a few, punish the dangerous ones,
and forgive the balance. I have told my brother fire-eaters
that would have been better." (Vol. 6: p. 113.)

He is quite unconscious that the citizens of Massachusetts,
while they would not like that number of *ignorant* voters cast
upon them, would be very nearly indifferent whether they took
one hundred thousand of Georgia's ignorant *negroes* or a like
number of her ignorant *whites*, which that State could furnish
with equal readiness. Mr. ATKINS, before referred to as a very
thoughtful Southern man, had dimly discerned this fact, as is
shown in his testimony (Vol. 9: p. 958, *Reports*):—

" *Question.* As to the ruling sentiment in your State, is there not among all the respectable men in the State the same horror in regard to cruelty towards the black race and to outrages upon them that there would be in any other community ?

" *Ans.* If you will pardon me, I think the question betrays a want of understanding on that subject. I do not think the white men here look upon the negro as he is looked upon in some of the other States. When he was a slave they looked upon him as a chattel; they did not pretend to disguise that fact. Now they look upon him as something worse than a chattel— more like a bad animal that they must fear. The feeling crops out in a great many ways, showing that they look upon him as something different from what they before considered him. Before, they considered him as a gentle animal that they would take care of for his services; at least that was my feeling, and my father had that feeling, and I think it was the feeling generally among the people where I was raised. Now, in the place of that kindly feeling of the master there is a feeling of bitterness, a feeling that the negro is a sort of instinctive enemy of ours. And I do not think that feeling leaves the mind in a condition to treat him as a white man would be treated under similar circumstances. For instance, a gentleman in this city with whom I was talking a couple of weeks ago on the subject of our country generally, and particularly of our servants, said that we never could get along in the condition we were until we could have our servants kept in subordination and made to feel a proper humility before us. I replied to him that I had none of that feeling; that I did not want any man to feel humble before me; all that I wanted of a man was that he should do his duty and treat me respectfully, and I would treat him so; all I ask of a man is to recognize our relations and to perform his part well. My friend said he felt differently; that he desired a servant should be humble, just as the negroes were in times of slavery. That was his language. That very same week I entered into conversation with one of our jurors. He was telling me of his practice in South Carolina; how he had threatened negroes, had "bully-ragged" them, to use his own expression. He did not seem to think he was betraying anything extraordinary, but I do not think he would talk to a white man so. I think many of our people are inclined to ill-treat a negro more than they would a white man. I do not think there is any question about that.

" Q. Then, after all, you believe that the perturbations in society here are caused by a want of adjustment between the races ?

" A. Yes, sir.

" Q. That is the foundation of your troubles ?

" A. I do not think there is any doubt about it."

## CHAPTER XI.

THE CAUSES, CHARACTER, AND CONSEQUENCES OF THE KU-KLUX
ORGANIZATION.—A RECAPITULATION.

### The Causes.

THE reader who has followed us thus far has obtained some faint idea of the most wonderful combination of armed men for unlawful purposes which the civilized world has ever known. There have been conspiracies and revolutions more desperate and daring, but none so widespread, secret, universal among so great a people, and above all so successful. It may be well to review briefly in conclusion the causes, character, purpose, and effect of this remarkable organization.

The cause—or to speak more accurately, the occasion—of its rise and sudden growth is, no doubt, somewhat complex. Its objective point was the overthrow of what is known as the reconstructionary legislation, including the abrogation or nullification of the thirteenth, fourteenth, and fifteenth amendments to the Federal Constitution; and the cause of its sudden spread was the almost universal hostility, on the part of the whites of the South, to this legislation and its *anticipated* results. For it should be kept constantly in mind that this organization was instituted and *in active operation in at least four States before a single one of the reconstructed State governments had been organized.*

### Effects of the War.

The reason of this hostility is not difficult to assign, though its elements are almost as various as the classes of mind and temperament which were affected by it. With some it was probably exasperation and chagrin at the results of the war. No doubt this was the chief incentive acting upon the minds of those who originally instituted in Tennessee this famous scheme of secret resistance to the policy of the government. Not only the sting of defeat but the shame of punishment without its terror combined to induce those who had cast all their hopes of honor and success upon the Confederate cause to lend themselves to any thing that would tend to humiliate the power which, in addition to the fact of conquest, had endeavored to impose upon them the stigma of treason. There is no doubt that the disfranchisement of those who had engaged in rebellion—or a "war for secession," as they prefer that it should be termed—was almost universally deemed an insult and an outrage only second in infamy to the enfranchisement of the colored man, which was contemporaneous with it. It is a matter of the utmost difficulty for a Northern man to realize the strength and character of this sentiment at the South. It is well expressed by General J. B. GORDON, now U. S. Senator from Georgia:—

"We were greatly dissatisfied. We do not think that we have been fairly treated. . . . . We did not believe that the act of secession was treason; I do not believe it now. I do not expect ever to believe it. I never expect to *advocate* any more secession. I have given *that* up; but I do not believe it was treason.

"Q. You did not believe it was treason when you originally advocated it ?                          .

"A. No, sir; and I do not believe it to-day; I never expect to believe it." (Vol. 6: p. 884.)

This is to-day the sentiment of nine tenths of the men who served in the Confederate army, or aided and abetted the side of the South in that struggle. It is a feeling, too, which is espoused with added intensity by the sons and daughters of these men, the young men and young women of the South. It is as if a personal affront were offered to the parent in the view and presence of the child. The parent might trace it to its source and in part condone its motive, but the child never will. It must be remembered, too, that these younger ones were reared in the very vortex of seething passions, in the midst of warfare and bitter and humiliating defeat. The specious casuistry by which this notion is supported satisfies the typical

Southern man that the advocacy of secession and the war in its support were not only righteous and praiseworthy, but were also in real truth done in support and vindication of the true theory of our Constitution and government. Strange as it may seem, instead of having any regret for his part in provoking and waging the war, the average Southern man believes most solemnly that he fought in a holy cause and in support of the true theory of constitutional liberty. He regards the North not only as having been the aggressor as regards the institution of Slavery, but also as having subverted and destroyed the Constitution which he fought to maintain and preserve in its original purity. That he should be stigmatized for such an act very naturally engendered a rancorous hate towards his oppressor, and as this was not coupled with any fear of actual punishment, the step from hatred to revenge was but a short one which was readily and gladly taken.

### The "Carpet-Bagger" and "Caste."

This feeling was of course intensified by that pride of caste and prejudice of race, as well as the accustomed intolerance of diverse opinions which have already been considered as characteristic of the South. The antipathy to Northern men became laughable in its absurdity. The cry of "Carpet-bag" governments has been bandied about until it has become a synonym for oppression and infamy. That the reconstructionary governments were failures goes without denial; that incompetency and extravagance characterized them is a most natural result of their organization; but that any one of them was controlled by men of Northern birth is an idea of the sheerest folly and absurdity. In hardly one of them were there a score of officers, great and small, who were of Northern birth. A statement was published in 1870 in regard to the "carpet-baggers" of Georgia, and a number of the witnesses, such as the ex-Confederate Governor Brown, Judge Wright, and General Gordon, were asked as to its correctness, and each admitted its substantial truth, while its literal verity was avouched by others. The following is the statement alluded to:—

" As to the carpet-bag members of the Convention which framed the Reconstruction Constitution of Georgia, they were thirteen in number, while the whole membership of that body was one hundred and seventy-five, of whom thirty were colored men. Of these thirteen carpet-baggers, eleven were consistent members of Christian churches; and only two of the thirteen were given to profanity, intemperance, or the keeping of low company; the other eleven were recognized as good citizens of unexceptionable habits, and abilities in every case fair and in several brilliant. These thirteen carpet-baggers numbered among them more total abstainers from the use of intoxicating drinks than did the entire remainder of the Convention.

" The Legislature of Georgia elected in 1868 has been sharply criticised as grossly corrupt. Of its 214 members, but seven have become residents of the State since the war, and six of these seven carpet-baggers are moral and religious men. Yet we have often heard it charged that this (as is alleged) corrupt Legislature is controlled by " carpet-baggers." And the lobby, by which the Legislature is infested, contains but one prominent carpet-bagger, and that one, sufficiently notorious, has never, so far as is known to the writer, voted the Republican ticket or in any way contributed to its success. Not one of the State officers (unless indeed we except the State Superintendent of Education, who is an appointee of the government) is a carpet-bagger. Of the members of the XL. Congress elected in Georgia, two were carpet-baggers—both Christian men, and doing honor to the churches with which they were connected by an upright life and a steadfast regard for the rights of others. In the XLI. and XLII. Congresses no carpet-baggers from Georgia held a seat. As for county offices, not ten of them in the whole State are or have been filled by the class in question; and from the judiciary they are expressly excluded by the terms of the State Constitution, which requires a residence of five years as a qualification for judges, State's attorneys, or solicitors. I might add that carpet-baggers and negroes together have never numbered one sixth of the Legislature of Georgia."

The same is true in a similar proportion of the other States. In none did the influence of the " carpet-bagger" predominate. Very few of the officers were of Northern birth, and there is yet to be found a legislative body in which there were not more native white Republican and more native white Democrats than men of Northern birth. That most of the Northern men who were there were active and capable men is very true. That there were bad men among them there is no doubt. That they should be accused of all the evil and credited with none of the good is but natural, considering their situation as exponents of a hostile civilization and part of a victorious foe. That such charges should be credited against men simply because they were branded with the name of "carpet-baggers," by their brethren of the North living in States where *not one half* the officers and legislators are of native birth, is a matter not only of surprise but of shame.

The simple fact is that the North had been accustomed to be bullied and dictated to by the imaginary nondescript which it calls the "Southern gentleman" so long that it was almost impossible to avoid the tendency. This tendency is well expressed by Mr. Dibble in the pamphlet already quoted from (chap. vii), in the following language:—

"In the work of Herbert Spencer on the study of sociology, the author has written several chapters on Bias, and its influence on sociological beliefs. The Educational Bias; the Bias of Patriotism; the Class Bias; the Political Bias; the Theological Bias—he might have added a chapter on the Bias of Habit. It was the Bias of Habit, in a great degree, that led our Northern friends to shape their course and take their opinions during the period of reconstruction at the dictation of Southern leaders. For forty years before the war, these lordly gentlemen had stalked through the Halls of Congress, and all the channels of public observation, proclaiming the policy of the government; requiring that everything should be subordinate to the paramount interests of slavery. We lost sight of them during the war, and for a period after the war; they came upon the scene, however, after the enactment of the reconstruction laws, and they were not slow to discover that there existed a strong Bias of Habit in their favor in the North; and they made the most of it. I prefer not to follow the thought and observation out; it would be offensive; I myself am a Northern man by birth.

"Another, but a minor fact, going to explain the abandonment of the Southern Republicans by their Northern friends, was that there existed and still exists a general ignorance throughout the North of the true state of affairs in the South. The opponents of reconstruction controlled, in a great degree, the channels of information, and every event was colored and warped by the Southern press to deceive the country. Northern public men and private citizens, editors and correspondents, came and went away without comprehending the state of affairs which they witnessed. They were received hospitably, and they could not understand why it was that white Republicans were never found in the clubs, families, and public resorts to which they were introduced. They readily received the explanation which was tendered to them, that these carpet-baggers and scallawags, by reason of their immoralities and crimes, had become outcasts from all decent and respectable society. · · · · ·

"The North did not know that the crime of the white Republicans, as a class, for which they were condemned to unmitigated hatred and universal ostracism, was an offense against the prejudice of Caste."

### THE FEAR OF SERVILE INSURRECTION.

There was another cause for the sudden spread of the Klan throughout the South which it is hard for the Northern mind to appreciate. Despite the marvelous peacefulness and long-suffering of the colored race, the people of the South had come to entertain an instinctive horror of servile or negro insurrections. Under the old slave *régime* this feeling was no doubt, in a measure, the product of that conscience which "doth make cowards of us all;" for it is unlikely that one could practice that "sum of all villainies," as Wesley vigorously phrased the description of Slavery, without doing violence to that moral mentor. It was, however, much more the result of that demagogic clamor which had for fifty years or more dwelt with inexhaustible clamor upon the inherent and ineradicable savageness of the gentle and docile race that was held in such carefully guarded subjection. This feeling was manifested and deepened in those days by the terrible enactments in which the "Black Codes" of the South abounded, all designed to check disobedience of any kind, and especially that which might lead to organized resistance. The constant repetition of this bugbear of a servile insurrection as a defensive argument for the institution of Slavery had impressed every man, woman, and child at the South with a vague and unutterable horror of the ever-anticipated day when the docile African should be transformed into a demon too black for hell's own purlieus.

Year after year, for more than one generation, the Southern heart had been fired by the depiction of these horrors. In every political campaign the opposing orators upon the stump had striven to outdo each other in portraying the terrors of San Domingo and the Nat Turner insurrection, until they became words used to frighten children into good behavior. It came to be the chronic nightmare of the Southern mind. Every wayside bush hid an insurrection. Men were seized with a frenzy of unutterable rage at the thought, and women became delirious with apprehension at its mere mention. It was the root of much of that wild-eyed lunacy which bursts forth among the Southern people at the utterance of the magic slogan of to-day, "a war of races." There is no doubt but very many otherwise intelligent men and women are confirmed lunatics upon this subject. It has become a sort of holy horror with them. No greater offence can be given in a Southern household than to laugh at its absurdity. The race prejudice has been fostered and encouraged for political effect, until it has become a part of the mental and moral fiber of the people. There is no doubt but this feeling, taken in connection with the enfranchisement of the blacks, induced thousands of good citizens to ally themselves with the Klan upon the idea that they were acting in self-defence in so doing, and especially that they were securing the safety of their wives and children thereby. 52

### NEED OF A PATROL.

The old "patrol" system of the ante-bellum days and a devout belief in its necessity was also one of the active causes of the rapid spread of the Klan. This system was established by legislative enactment in all the Southern States. It varied somewhat in its details and in the powers conferred upon the patrolmen, or "patrollers" as they were popularly called. The purpose of the system, however, was declared to be "the preservation of order, and proper subordination among the colored population." The patrol generally consisted of a certain number of men, appointed for each captain's district or other local subdivision of the county, whose duty it was to patrol the public highway at night; to arrest and whip all negroes found beyond the limits of their masters' plantations after dark without a pass from the owner or overseer; to visit the "nigger quarters" on the plantations and see that no meetings or assemblies were held without the presence of a white man; and, in general, to exercise the severest scrutiny of the private life and demeanor of the subject-race. This system of espionage and the enforcement of the code designed for the control of the blacks without form of trial, had a great influence upon the mental status of both races. It deprived the person, house, and property of the freedman of all that sanctity which the law throws around the person, home, and possessions of the white man, in the minds of both the Caucasian and the African. The former came to believe that he had the right to trespass, and the latter that he must submit to this claim. As the spirit of the new era did not admit of such statutory espionage and summary correction of the black as had been admitted by all to be necessary in the days of Slavery, and as it was undeniable that emancipation had not changed the nature of the inferior race nor removed all grounds for disaffection on his part, it was but natural that there should be a general sentiment that some volunteer substitute was necessary. As the power to whip and chastise for any infraction of the code of slave-etiquette was conferred upon the patrol, it was equally natural that they should regard the exercise of such authority by the Klan as not only necessary but quite a fit and proper thing to be done by them.

53

## THE BRUTALITY OF SLAVERY.

The chief ground of doubt at the North in regard to the atrocities of the Klan, the Bull-dozers, and the Rifle Clubs, is that it seems altogether incredible that the being so long and loudly self-vaunted as the very incarnation of all that is noble, generous, brave, and Christianlike—the ideal "Southern gentleman—" should assent to or engage in such atrocities. The trouble about this reasoning is that the "Southern gentleman," according to the Northern conception of him, is an almost

mythical personage. The North has mistaken the terms used
in self-description by the Southern aristocrat, who was at no
time economical of adjectives. The perfect gentleman of
the South is very apt, along with many splendid qualities
and noble impulses, to possess others which at the North
would be accounted very reprehensible. He is simply like
other men, good according to the style and measure of his
era and surroundings. In the old days a man might be a
perfect gentleman and yet a cruel master, a keen speculator in
human flesh, the sire of his own slaves,—and literally a dealer
in his own flesh and blood. The Northern mind was horrified
at such a combination. Yet it should not have been. The
greatest evil of slavery was that it brutified the feelings of the
master-race and lowered and degraded their estimate of humanity. The human form divine was cheapened and made
common to their eyes by the constant spectacle of its degradation.
It is true that it was most usually in ebon hue; but, as the
process of amalgamation went on, the color-line as a test of
slavery faded away, and in every county of the South the
spectacle became a frequent one of a slave as white in cuticle
and regular in lineament as the master, and not unfrequently
bearing the unmistakable marks of the same paternity. The
necessities of this relation made a brutality which sickens the
unaccustomed heart a thing of frequent contemplation. Even
laying aside all estimate of the frailty of nature and the ex-
cesses of passion, the very fact that the life and limb of the
slave were at the unquestioned and unquestionable disposal of
the master must convince any thoughtful mind of the terrible
strain which was imposed upon Southern humanity. The
matter of surprise is not that they became so unconsciously
brutal and barbarous as regards the colored man, but that so
much real kindness survived the terrible ordeal.                          54

It should be remembered that the institution of Slavery so
warped and marred the common-law that grave and reverend—
yea, conscientious, learned, and Christian men announced from
the bench, with all the solemn sanction of the judicial ermine,
doctrines with regard to the master's power over the person of

the slave which are now considered barbarous and unlawful when applied to his brute possessions. In some States it was held that slavery vested the master with absolute power over the life of the slave; and, in all, that he might kill him to enforce obedience or to punish insolence. It is true that the slave was protected to a certain extent from the violence and passion of those not entitled to exercise mastery over him, but that was merely or chiefly for the sake of the master whose property he was.

This influence affected the so-called best classes of the South far more than it did the middle and lower classes, simply because they were more exposed to its influence. There were, indeed, many instances of brutified overseers, but as a rule the lower classes of the South were not in a position to see or experience so much of the evil effects of Slavery as the highest and best. These latter made and administered the laws, and the brutality of those laws reflected itself on their hearts and in their lives. Their lives were not all brutal, but they looked with coolness on brutality.

For a hundred years the following was one of the laws of South Carolina, "for the better ordering and governing of negroes and slaves":—

"*Be it further enacted,* &c., That every slave above sixteen years of age that shall run away and so continue for the space of twenty days at one time, shall, by his master's, mistress's or overseer's procurement, for the *first* offence be publicly whipped not exceeding forty lashes; and in case such negro or slave shall run away a *second* time and so continue for the space of twenty days, he or she so offending shall be branded with the letter R on the right cheek. And in case such negro or slave shall run away the *third* time and shall so continue for the space of thirty days, he or she so offending shall for the *third* offence be severely whipped, not exceeding forty lashes, and shall have one of his ears cut off. And in case such male negro or slave shall run away a *fourth* time, he so offending for the *fourth* offence shall be gelt. And if a female slave shall run away the *fourth* time she shall be severely whipped" [no limit] "and be branded on the left cheek with the letter R" [the right being already so ornamented for the second offence] "and have her left ear cut off" [the right having already been cut off for the third offence]. And in case any negro or slave shall run away the *fifth* time and shall so continue for the space of thirty days at one time, such slave shall be tried before two justices of the peace and three freeholders, and by them being declared guilty of the offence, it shall be lawful for them to order *the cord of the slave's leg to be cut above the heel*, or else to *pronounce sentence of death* upon said slave, at the discretion of said justices." (Statutes at Large, 1835, p. 359.)

55

Can any outrage committed by the Klan exceed this solemnly enacted barbarity?

Yet this was not cruelty, nor were the men who enacted it savages. They were the first gentlemen of South Carolina—cultivated, rich, refined, hospitable, brave, and kind. It was not done from any desire to torture the slave, but simply to protect the Institution. It was not cruelty but simply *indifference*, as to the slave, *as a person* and tender regard for him as property. Should it be matter of surprise that the gentlemen who enacted and administered this and other laws of similar tone could countenance, approve, and promote the most barbarous acts of the Klan? The masked night-riders but did without law what the law so recently had authorized them to do without judge or jury!

That the course of these organizations should be marked with blood and torture is therefore but natural, and the "Southern gentleman" is just as much a possibility under the mask of a Ku-Klux as he was "in the good old times when we *had* a Republic" and drove his slaves afield under the sanction of such laws as we have cited. Ku-Klux cruelty and outrage was but the natural fruit of slavery's barbarity ! The men who engaged in both these acts were simply no better and no worse than their surroundings and training made them.

It has been thought by some that the callousness attributed in "A Fool's Errand" to the murderers of John Walters, in admitting his murder but indignantly denying the imputation of having stolen money from his person *for their personal benefit* and boldly claiming that it was used solely and sacredly to promote the interests of the party with which the murderers acted, was beyond the limit and range of even the most hardened and distorted human nature. The incident is closely paralleled in the noted case of the Yazoo election for sheriff.

The facts of that case are briefly these. In the campaign of 1875, there was an extensive "White League" raid made upon the Republicans of Yazoo County, Mississippi, some of whom were killed and others driven off. Among those who were killed was a member of the Legislature named Patterson, who was seized and hung by a Ku-Klux gang, having on his person at the time of his seizure a large sum of money which was never recovered by his family or heard of in fact until 1879, when one of the leaders of this murderous band became a candidate for sheriff, against the regular nominee of the Democratic party. As soon as he did so, Dr. P. J. McCormick, who was Chairman of the Democratic Committee of Yazoo County in 1875, published a card declaring that Dixon was the leader of the mob which hung Patterson, and that he converted to his own use the money which was on Patterson's person when seized. To this charge Dixon replied through the columns of the *Yazoo Herald*, in which it appeared as an advertisement, by the following card:

### A CARD TO THE PUBLIC.

"Owing to certain reports now in circulation that Patterson, a member of the Republican Legislature, who was hanged in the eventful campaign of 1875, had a considerable sum of money on his person, and that said money was used for my own benefit, I feel in honor bound to vindicate myself, although I deplore to refer to the past, as it will bring before the public many of our best citizens. I will briefly state that said money, and larger sums, were raised and used to defray the current expenses of the campaign, and to stuff the ballot-boxes, if necessary; to purchase certificates of election for two officers now holding offices of trust and emolument in our county. I have in my possession the necessary proof, and if called on will furnish it.          H. M. DIXON."

To this Dr. P. J. McCormick responded evasively, declaring that "*the constituted authorities* of the Democratic party had nothing to do with the raising of said money or the use made of said money."

To this Dixon again responded by another advertisement in the same journal on the 6th of June, 1879, as follows:

"*Editor Herald:* In response to the card of Dr. P. J. McCormick, that appeared in the *Sentinel*, I will state that I did not assert in my card that the constituted Democratic authorities had any connection with the Patterson affair, nor did I charge that the ballot-boxes were stuffed.

"I again say that the supposed Patterson money was used to defray current expenses of the eventful campaign of 1875.

"I further state that $3000 was paid as a bribe to have the ballot-boxes stuffed, if necessary, and to issue certificates of election to the Democratic candidates; that Dr. P. J. McCormick was Chairman of the Democratic Executive Committee at the time, and was a party to the contract. I have in my possession the necesary receipt to show who received the $3000; also the false key to the ballot-box.

"I consider that my conduct throughout the canvass of 1875 was fully indorsed by all Democratic citizens, and I do not fear that my character will suffer by any cowardly attack made for a political purpose.

"Respectfully,     H. M. DIXON."

It will be observed that the charge of murder is treated as of very little moment; that the taking of the money from the body of the murdered man is politely termed "raising" money by both, and that the charge of having applied it to secure unlawful and corrupt election returns is openly made and only evasively answered.

The result of the Yazoo affair is another good illustration of the spirit pervading Southern society, which will not permit dissent from its views nor tolerate the presence of any man of any party who appeals to the colored voter for political aid. Dixon, as will be remembered, was shot down upon the streets in open day by a man who had previously declared his intention to do so, and after having been threatened by an armed mob who demanded his withdrawal from the canvass on the ground that any one who asked the support of colored men as against a Democratic nominee was precipitating a race-conflict. Upon the matter being laid before the Grand Jury of the county, the bill was promptly ignored; upon what ground it would be hard to guess, unless it was that the gen-

tlemen composing the Grand Jury thought it a praiseworthy
act to assassinate any one who dared to appeal to colored voters
for political preferment against the will of the white voters of
the county.

These facts are not noted to awaken any animosity toward
these men. They are no more in fault for the training which
Slavery gave them than the rest of the nation, which protected
and encouraged its continuance and growth for so many years
—a nation which long refused to listen or give credence to its
daily enormities because it was impossible that Southern
57  Christian gentlemen should engage in or permit them.

### THE CONTROLLING POWERS.

The idea which has prevailed that the Ku-Klux were simply
rough, lawless, irresponsible young rowdies is a singularly absurd reflection on the "best" classes—their power and inherited
authority over their poorer neighbors.     The minority which
forced an overwhelming majority into what the victims themselves termed "the rich man's war and the poor man's fight,"
is still omnipotent in the domain of Southern public opinion.
If they had disapproved of the doings of these men, the Klan
would have shrivelled before the first breath of denunciation.
But that breath never came with any earnestness or sincerity of
tone until the object of the organization, the *destruction of the
negro's political power*, had been fully accomplished.     It is a
reflection on the power of the best citizens to indulge the idea
that the rabble could do any thing in opposition to their wishes.
Professedly, they feebly "deplored" what was done, but in
fact they either directly encouraged or were discreetly silent.
That thousands of them loaned their horses for poor men to
ride upon raids is just as certain as that they should put sub-
58  stitutes into the army under "the twenty-nigger law."

Another thing which shows that the claim made in extenuation
—that it was merely the work of rough spirits of the lower classes—is a libel on the common people of the South, is the fact
that the best classes never prosecuted nor denounced these acts,
but were always their apologists and defenders.     Besides that,

they kept the secrets of the Klan better than the Masons have ever kept the mysteries of their craft. It was an open secret in families and neighborhoods. Ladies met together in sewing-circles to make the disguises. Churches were used as places of assembly. Children were intrusted with secrets which will make them shudder in old age. Yet the freemasonry of a common impulse kept them as true as steel. As a rule, the only ones who flinched were a few of the more unfortunate or more cowardly of its members. Not a woman or a child lisped a syllable that might betray the fatal secret. It was a holy trust which the Southern cause had cast upon them, and they would have died rather than betray it.

The fact has been overlooked, too, that whenever positive information has been obtained as to the membership of the Klan, it has been shown to have have had its full proportion of the best classes. Two judges, two sheriffs, one State solicitor, one leading editor, four members of the Legislature, one Congressman, and numerous lawyers and planters and professional men, are shown by the testimony in *one* State alone, to have been among its members. The confessions of members showed the officers and leading men of the Klans always to have been men of standing and influence in their communities.

It is more than probable that many men of standing and influence refrained from becoming actual members in order that they might truthfully deny all knowledge of it. A gentleman who now occupies a high judicial position in one of the Southern States said to the writer (about the time when "the bottom fell out"), "Well, I never was a member. Somebody sent me a constitution and ritual, and a gentleman explained the signs, &c., to me; but I was never a member, and always refused to listen to any statement as to who was at its head in the county, etc. I didn't wish to know." Why he did not wish to know he did not say, but the reader may well imagine.

There is no sort of doubt that it originated with the best classes of the South, was managed and controlled by them, and was at all times under their direction. It was their creature and their agent to work out their purposes and ends. It was just as much their movement as was the war of rebellion, and animated by similar motives.

## The Consequences.

The immediate and most notable consequence of this movement was, of course, the overthrow of the reconstructed governments, the suppression of the negro as a potential political factor, and the re-establishment of the old rule of a minority instead of that of the whole people which had been instituted by national legislation. The more remote and occult results are not difficult to determine. A moment's consideration will place them in clear and indubitable relief in every mind.

1. The operations of the Klan have demonstrated that national law is powerless as against the public sentiment of any State, and may safely be defied by any one acting in accord with that sentiment. This is illustrated in Mr. Hogan's article in the *International Review* as follows:—

" A single Democratic juryman will hold out for life, and disagreements are the inevitable consequence of every indictment for such an offence. Judge Northrup, a native South Carolinian and District Attorney of that district, has at present under indictment over five hundred Democrats for election frauds, and stands ready to secure the indictment of as many more, including the most prominent men in the State and the Democratic Executive Committee. This officer informs me that the proof of their guilt is plainer than the writing on the wall at the feast of Belshazzar; but that Chief Justice Waite himself on the bench, and Mr. Evarts and Gen. Devens prosecuting, could not secure their conviction before a jury of the State."

59

Every one who has been at all familiar with the state of feeling there knows that this wholesale system of fraud is a matter of boastful jest with the very best of citizens. They do not deem it a matter of wrong or evil, because, as they say, "it prevents nigger-rule." This public opinion is the safeguard of any unlawful act having a like object in view.

2. It has shown conspiracy and revolution to be the shortest, easiest, and surest method of obtaining public honor and prefer-

ment. Disguise it as we may endeavor to do, the fact still remains that a vast majority of all the officers in any of the
Southern States owe their present position either to their prominence in the war of the rebellion or their activity and zeal in
the Ku-Klux conspiracy.

3. It has clearly proved that the ballot is no efficient protector of personal or political rights against the sentiment of
caste or race-prejudice ; that mere numbers cannot sustain
themselves in power, unless they have also intelligence, property,
and experience; nor can they protect themselves by any legal
or peaceful means against a minority having these advantages.

4. It has shown that the sole ground of sectional hostility
between North and South was not removed by the emancipation of the blacks. In fact, it has shown that, in spirit and
education, character and purpose, the two sections are more
widely separated, more entirely distinct, than had theretofore
been supposed.

5. It has ceased simply because it had nothing more to feed
upon. With the suppression of the negro and Republican
vote, and the establishment of the old minority rule, its purpose was accomplished. There was nothing more to be done.
As a consequence, what is termed "peace" has succeeded to the
reign of violence and terror. But it is the peace of force, of
suppression, of subverted right, of trampled and defied law.

6. And, finally, the spirit and animus of this organization
still remain. It is not dead, but sleepeth only. Whenever occasion shall serve, it may be again invoked by the bold political
buccaneers who lead and control the sentiment of its members,
and required to do their bidding and subserve their purposes.

That this is true is shown by a thousand constantly recurring
indices, of which a few must suffice. Any one who will cast
his memory back but three years will recall with what marvelous readiness armed forces sprang into existence in Louisiana and South Carolina,—not wild undisciplined, disorganized
and frenzied mobs; nothing of the kind; but cool, organized
battalions, carrying the most improved repeating arms, obedient to orders and subservient to discipline as any army which

ever mustered on the continent. *Apropos* of this subject, Mr. Hogan writes:—

" South Carolina, in 1876, resembled a military camp. Indeed, the young men of the State to-day are far better educated as calvary men than as business men, and in shaving potatoes and snuffing candles at ten paces, than in 'the three R's.' At a certain signal in 1876, as many as 40,000 well-armed men could have been assembled in twelve hours. This military establishment is still available, and the spirit of the old rifle-clubs still lives with it."

This, it should be remembered, is the view of one of Gov. Hampton's admirers, in February, 1880.

Even as these lines are written there comes further proof that the spirit which has been delineated is yet active and virulent. According to a newspaper printed in Aberdeen, Mississippi, the School Board of that county has just passed the following resolution:

" Be it resolved, That it is the opinion of the Executive Committee that there should no longer be any radical school-teacher employed in the capacity of public-school teacher in the county of Monroe, and that the Superintendent of Education be specially requested to decline giving any radical a certificate as teacher."

Upon this, the Superintendent has issued the following document, to be signed by each applicant before getting certificate:

" I certify that I have been a Democrat, and that I will hereafter support the candidates of the Democratic party and work with that party."

" The above is required before I approve a contract.

_____  _____

                                                    *Superintendent.*"

Still further evidence of how hard it is for a "nigger" to get a "white man's chance" in the South may be found in the remarkable emigration of colored men to the Northwest which has become so striking as to be termed an "Exodus."

But enough has been said to give some sense of the situation. In conclusion, the author desires to re-state the fact which he has endeavored constantly to keep before the reader's mind, that the foregoing narrative and the facts which have been given are not intended to awaken hostility or inspire prejudice; but only to provoke inquiry, invite investigation, and stimulate thought. It is apparent to all that the evils which now afflict the body-politic arising out of the recent past can be cured only by a thorough comprehension of their nature, tendency and extent. Before the North and South can actually become one people in spirit, and look forward to a permanently united government and a common destiny, they must understand and appreciate each other. The antagonistic moral forces must be fully apprehended in order that moral influences as well as political power may be exerted to secure their reconciliation or the extinction of that which is defective and erroneous.

The moral, physical, intellectual, and financial power of the country resides at the North, but it should not be forgotten that more than one third of the political power resides at the South—where forty-five *per cent* of the voters cannot read their ballots,—and that *less* than one third of the population of the country embraces *more* than two thirds of the illiteracy.

These briefly stated facts, taken in connection with those which have been given before, must show to every thoughtful man the necessity of making an immediate study of this matter and acting at once in regard to it. Instead of having been eliminated from politics, the "Southern Question" presents now what is perhaps its most dangerous, because its most difficult and delicate phase. That change must come, that the present situation of affairs can not endure for any great length of time, is certain. What shall take its place is a most important question which the American people, and especially the people of the North, are called upon to answer.

The answer which has already been suggested in these pages may be again referred to here, and the question asked once more, whether any thing can make the South an honored and equal partner of the North, except such an *education of the masses* as shall make that beautiful portion of our land genuinely "democratic" and truly "republican."

That something has been done to remedy this evil is very true. Northern charity and missionary zeal at first poured an army of zealous teachers into the South to teach the Freedmen; almost all the religious denominations of the North have established and to-day support very creditable institutions of learning there; the beneficence of Peabody dispenses its blessing to those who are at once fortunate and worthy; State appropriation has done something, and individual enterprise something more. Yet it is doubtful if the advance has been sufficient to show any decrease in the average of illiteracy given by the last census. In this matter, too, it should be remembered that it is always well to look outside of mere reports. School statistics are even more easily "cooked" than election returns. That may be termed a school which is quite unworthy of the name. And we shall find the fact to be that those of the purest lives, whose exertions have resulted in erecting institutions worth thousands upon thousands of dollars for the use of Freedmen in Southern cities, by appeals to Northern charity, and who have given their lives to the conduct of these schools, are as thoroughly ostracized as ever. Men may visit the schools and make pretty speeches and sympathize with them, and now and then small appropriations may be voted for their support; but the Northern men and women who teach in them know that it is none the less a fact that they may not cross the mystic pale of the life around them. They are *anathema maranatha* because they have degraded their caste by association with pariahs, even though it be only in the attempt to elevate them.

There are some Southerners, no doubt many, who deplore this fact; but there are few, ah, so very few! who deplore it deeply enough to stand up against it or seriously fight the prevalent opinion. The report of a Superintendent of Education in one of those States speaks with touching tenderness of the duty of the State and the people toward the ignorant colored man. He is a minister of the Gospel, and one wishes to believe his words, "for the very word's sake." In the same city is a minister of the same denomination, a graduate of a New England college and seminary. He has begged from Northern givers money to erect the finest school buildings in the State. His genreous wife has cast in her dowry to complete the needed amount. It is held by trustees, and he has no pecuniary interest therein. For fifteen years he has turned out, perhaps, the most thorough and unpretentious colored teachers of the South—hundreds upon hundreds of them. The Superintendent "deplores prejudice and opposition to education;" yet he would as soon think of committing suicide as of inviting that devoted teacher and his intelligent and accomplished wife to his family board. Not one of Southern birth in that whole cityful has ever done it!

But however willing the South might be to educate her masses, it would be both impossible and unjust for her to do so. She ought not to be required to do so if able; and she is not able. The mass of ignorance is so great, and the taxable values so reduced, that adequate school facilities are an impossibility for a generation, if left to the Southern States alone.

Two bits of testimony bring us food for thought—the one a petition for national aid and the other a protest against it. Dr. Sears, the learned, patriotic, and philanthropic agent of the Peabody Fund, petitions for proceeds of the sales of public lands to be devoted to curing Southern ignorance. The *New Orleans Picayune*, in commenting on this, declares: " *The masses* of the Southern people do not desire school help from the Federal Government in any form."

But the Nation, it must never be forgotten, is responsible for the creation of this mass of ignorance by the protection and encouragement which it extended to Slavery, and therefore has a duty in the matter which ought not to be shirked.

If this volume shall in any manner tend to aid in the performance of this duty, in directing and stimulating thought and inquiry and thereby solving the great riddle which has been put before this generation, the author will feel that the severe experience on which it is based was by no means " A Fool's Errand."

That it will do so he thoroughly believes, and he looks forward with confidence to a time when North and South alike shall thank him for the bitter but wholesome truths which he has laid before them for consideration.

# NOTES

---

1. See *Report and Testimony of the Select Committee of the United States Senate to Investigate the Causes of the Removal of the Negroes from the Southern States to the Northern States* (3 vols.; Washington, D.C., 1880), in *Senate Reports,* 46th Cong., 2nd Sess., No. 693. For the history of black migration, see Nell Irvin Painter, *Exodusters: Black Migration to Kansas After Reconstruction* (New York, 1976).

2. Tourgée's concept of these disparities is in accordance with recent scholarship. For example, see Otto H. Olsen (ed.), *Reconstruction and Redemption in the South* (Baton Rouge, 1980).

3. The basis of representation was more diverse than Tourgée suggests. Use of the federal ratio (counting blacks as three-fifths of a person) was common, but the number of whites or qualified voters was utilized in most of the upper South, and there were other variations. See Ralph A. Wooster's *The People in Power: Courthouse and Statehouse in the Lower South, 1850–1860* (Knoxville, 1969), and *Politicians, Planters, and Plain Folk: Courthouse and Statehouse in the Upper South, 1850–1860* (Knoxville, 1975).

4. A readmission act was passed in June, 1868, and the first four states were admitted during July.

5. Tourgée's fears would be confirmed before the end of

the century by intensified racism and a wave of lynchings. See C. Vann Woodward, *The Strange Career of Jim Crow* (3rd rev. ed.; New York, 1974), Ch. 3.

6. Nathan Bedford Forrest does not appear to have initiated the Ku Klux Klan, but he joined it soon after its inauguration and was elected its Grand Wizard in 1867. Forrest was in command of the Confederate attack on Fort Pillow on April 12, 1864, that culminated in what some scholars have judged a massacre. John Cimprich and Robert C. Mainfort, Jr. (eds.), "Fort Pillow Revisited: New Evidence About an Old Controversy," *Civil War History,* XXVIII (1982), 293–306.

7. The more popular derivation of Ku Klux relates it to the Greek word *kuklos,* meaning circle, and sometimes also to the southern college fraternity Kuklos Adelphon. Allen W. Trelease, *White Terror: The Ku Klux Klan Conspiracy and Southern Reconstruction* (New York, 1971), 4.

8. From March 15, 1867, to March 16, 1869, George H. Thomas, a Union general from Virginia who acquired fame as the Rock of Chickamauga, was in command of the Department of the Cumberland, which included Kentucky and Tennessee.

9. Walter Brock was a Union man who served in the Georgia legislature from 1863 to 1871.

10. George R. Ashburn's assassination was the first Klan outrage to be reported outside Tennessee, and gained widespread publicity. A Georgian who fled the state during the war and joined the Union army, Ashburn became a vigorous and effective Reconstructionist, with a devoted black following. Shortly after midnight, a band of over thirty disguised men broke into his home and shot and killed him. Trelease, *White Terror,* 76–77.

11. Trelease concludes there were 550,000. *White Terror,* 45.

12. It was not agreed that citizenship conferred the right to vote upon blacks any more than it did upon women. It was this fact that necessitated the Fifteenth Amendment.

13. Tennessee ratified the Fourteenth Amendment on July 11 and 12, 1866, and was accepted back into the Union by Congress on July 23, 1866. It was never subject to the Reconstruction Acts of 1867.

14. *Testimony Taken by the Joint Select Committee to Inquire into the Condition of Affairs in the Late Insurrectionary States* (13 vols.; Washington, D.C., 1872), I, 83, hereinafter cited as KKK Report.

15. Generals George H. Thomas, Edward R. S. Canby, Joseph J. Reynolds, Philip H. Sheridan, and Alfred H. Terry all served as district commanders in the postwar South. Edward Hatch's account appears in "Testimony Taken by the Sub-Committee of Elections in Louisiana," *House Miscellaneous Documents,* 41st Cong., 2nd Sess., No. 154, pp. 28–41. Hatch testified that his atrocity figures were taken only from the parishes adjoining New Orleans, and estimated that the actual number killed was closer to 900 than to the 297 specific killings he reported (pp. 32, 39). While many generals, including Terry, Howard, and Nelson A. Miles, corroborated this terrible assessment, others disagreed. In November, 1869, just prior to an eruption of Klan activity, Henry W. Halleck concluded, "Although there may be special organizations of outlaws in particular localities under the name of Ku Klux, I am of the opinion that no such general organization now exists in the southern States." *House Executive Documents,* 41st Cong., 2nd Sess., No. 1, p. 78. General Oliver O. Howard concluded a month earlier that "the reports of murders, assaults and outrages of every description were so numerous and so full of horrible details, that at times one was inclined to believe the whole white population was engaged in a war of extermination against the blacks."

*House Executive Documents,* 41st Cong., 2nd Sess., No. 142, p. 14. Ted Tunnell accepts comparable estimates of the number killed and notes that the Republican vote declined from 65,000 votes in April, to 33,000 in November of that year. Tunnell, *Crucible of Reconstruction: War, Radicalism, and Race in Louisiana, 1862–1877* (Baton Rouge, 1984), 153–57.

16. KKK Report, I, 19–21.

17. Abram Colby, emancipated from slavery before the war, was elected twice to the Georgia legislature during Reconstruction.

18. H. D. Ingersoll, born in Gloucester, Massachusetts, came to Georgia in 1865 as a bookkeeper for a gold mining company.

19. Albion W. Tourgée, *A Fool's Errand by One of the Fools* (New York, 1879), Ch. 31. The killing of Uncle Jerry was modeled in part on the actual murder of Wyatt Outlaw, on which see Otto H. Olsen, "The Ku Klux Klan: A Study in Reconstruction Politics and Propaganda," *North Carolina Historical Review,* XXXIX (1962), 354–55.

20. Augustus R. Wright.

21. KKK Report, XIII, 35–36, 41.

22. Richardson was a carpenter but was involved in a partnership with his brother in a grocery.

23. The testimony regarding Stafford was given by Tunis G. Campbell of Georgia, a black from the North, a minister of the African Methodist Episcopal Zion Church, and a state senator. KKK Report, VII, 851, 857. Campbell's career may be followed in Edmund L. Drago, *Black Politicians and Reconstruction in Georgia* (Baton Rouge, 1982).

24. The buildings were burned and the men driven off. KKK Report, VII, 1048–49.

25. KKK Report, IX, 1048–54.

26. Joseph H. Speed's testimony occurs in KKK Report, VIII, 413–27. Portions of his career are described in Sarah Woolfolk Wiggins, *The Scalawag in Alabama Politics, 1865–1881* (University, Ala., 1977).

27. As a superior court judge in North Carolina, Tourgée was directly involved in taking such confessions. Related confessions may also be found in *Third Annual Message of W. W. Holden . . . Nov. 1870* (Raleigh, 1870), and *Trial of William W. Holden, Governor of North Carolina . . .* (3 vols.; Raleigh, 1871).

28. This name appears variously as Cornelous and Cornelius. There was no mention of a death threat in this testimony, but for such threats, see KKK Report, IX, 1198, 1200, 1202, 1233.

29. The excerpts that follow are taken from sections of the laws of South Carolina and Louisiana, which may be found in Edward McPherson (ed.), *The Political History of the United States of America During the Period of Reconstruction* (1875; rpr. New York, 1969), 36, 43–44.

30. Black behavior was more complex than the views of Tourgée and General John Brown Gordon suggest. Although there is general agreement that violent resistance by blacks, outside their service in the Union army, was rare, that policy reflected the realities of power and circumstance as well as possible good will. For discussion of the ambiguities involved, see William E. B. Du Bois, *Black Reconstruction in America: An Essay Toward a History of the Part Which Black Folk Played in the Attempt to Reconstruct Democracy in America, 1860–1880* (1935; rpr. New York, 1964), Ch. 4; Herbert Aptheker, *American Negro Slave Revolts* (New York, 1943); Eugene Genovese, *Roll, Jordan, Roll: The World the Slaves Made* (New York, 1974); Leon F. Litwack, *Been in the Storm So Long: The Aftermath of Slavery* (New

York, 1979); and Ira Berlin, Joseph P. Reidy, and Leslie P. Rowland (eds.), *Freedom: A Documentary History of Emancipation, 1861–1867. Series II. The Black Military Experience* (Cambridge, Eng., 1982).

31. KKK Report, VI, 327. For repudiations of the carpetbagger stereotype, see Richard N. Current, "Carpetbaggers Reconsidered," in David Pinckney and Theodore Ropp (eds.), *A Festschrift for Frederick B. Artz* (Durham, 1964); Current, *Three Carpetbag Governors* (Baton Rouge, 1967), and *Those Terrible Carpetbaggers* (New York, 1988); and Otto H. Olsen, *Carpetbagger's Crusade: The Life of Albion Winegar Tourgée* (Baltimore, 1965).

32. In this and all other instances the italics were added by Tourgée.

33. Tourgée erred in his identification. This was the testimony of Z. B. Hargrove, a native of Georgia and a former Confederate officer. A Democrat, he had served as a mayor and state legislator. KKK Report, VI, 73–75.

34. While the specific crimes discussed by Tourgée in this work did remain unpunished, a program of federal law and prosecution had led to the punishment of some Klansmen for their crimes. See Trelease, *White Terror*, 399–418. Trelease's final conclusions, however, do not differ substantially from those of Tourgée: "The federal government's enforcement campaign broke the back of the Ku Klux Klans, even if it failed to end them absolutely. On the other hand, it failed lamentably to bring more than a few Klansmen to justice after one of the most far-flung and persistent crime waves in American history. Southern violence now assumed other forms, almost as lethal, probably more effective, and certainly more lasting than the Ku Klux Klan." *Ibid.*, 418.

35. The index entry in Volume 6 is *Homicides*, not *Killings*.

36. The index entry for these names is *Killings.*

37. In contrast, the authority on Reconstruction in Mississippi concludes that opposition to black schools there was not a major motive of the Klan but that teachers attacked by the Klan were obnoxiously involved in politics. This would not obviate Tourgée's basic complaint, but it would indicate that only certain kinds of teaching were to be suppressed. William C. Harris, *The Day of the Carpetbagger: Republican Reconstruction in Mississippi* (Baton Rouge, 1979), 327–28, especially note 40. On the teaching of the freed slaves, see Willie Lee Rose, *Rehearsal for Reconstruction: The Port Royal Experiment* (New York, 1966); Ronald E. Butchart, *Northern Schools, Southern Blacks, and Reconstruction: Freedmen's Education, 1862–1875* (Westport, Conn., 1980); and Robert C. Morris, *Reading, 'Riting and Reconstruction: The Education of Freedmen in the South, 1861–1870* (Chicago, 1982).

38. Elias Hill was probably the model for the character Eliab Hill in Tourgée's *Bricks Without Straw. A Novel* (New York, 1880).

39. Stanley F. Horn claimed that it was the presentation of Allen P. Huggins' bloodstained shirt before Congress by Benjamin F. Butler that initiated the phrase "waving the bloody shirt." That story has been dismissed as a concoction. See Wyn Craig Wade, *The Fiery Cross: The Ku Klux Klan in America* (New York, 1987), 463.

40. The article by the Reverend E. Q. Fuller has not been located. The material he presents is located in the KKK Report as follows: William Jennings, VII, 1125–40; Wesley Shropshire, VI, 622–37; Caroline Smith, VII, 597–601; the Reverend A. S. Lakin, VIII, 111–59; William Dougherty, IX, 1022–42.

41. State senator Joseph Adkins was one of two Re-

publican legislators assassinated in Georgia in May, 1869. Alan Conway, *The Reconstruction of Georgia* (Minneapolis, 1966), 198.

42. In September, 1868, with the approval, or failure to vote, of a substantial number of white Republicans, twenty-five black legislators were expelled from the Georgia House of Representatives and two from the Senate solely because of their race. Although the state supreme court subsequently determined that they were entitled to their seats, they were reseated only through the ultimate intervention of Congress. See Elizabeth Studley Nathans, *Losing the Peace: Georgia Republicans and Reconstruction, 1865–1871* (Baton Rouge, 1968), 121–70.

43. Senator George Wallace, a black Republican, represented the Milledgeville region.

44. The opening sentence of this paragraph is an overstatement, which ignores, for example, the contributions of the South to the liberal ideology of the era of the American Revolution. Tourgée's focus, however, is upon the period of intense sectional struggle dating from about the 1820s, and many historians agree that the impact of abolitionism, the race question, and modernization did increasingly make intolerance a distinguishing characteristic of southern thought, one that Wilbur Cash called the "savage ideal." Wilbur J. Cash, *The Mind of the South* (New York, 1941). See also Bertram Wyatt-Brown, *Southern Honor: Ethics and Behavior in the Old South* (New York, 1941); Clement Eaton, *Freedom of Thought in the Old South* (Durham, 1940); and Robert F. Durden, *The Self-Inflicted Wound: Southern Politics in the 19th Century* (Lexington, Ky., 1985). For the related continuing debate over the extent to which the South was democratic or oligarchic, see especially Frank L. Owsley, *The Plain Folk of the Old South* (Baton Rouge,

1949); Ralph A. Wooster, *The People in Power: Courthouse and Statehouse in the Lower South, 1850–1860* (Knoxville, 1969), and *Politicians, Planters, and Plain Folk: Courthouse and Statehouse in the Upper South, 1850–1860* (Knoxville, 1975); J. Mills Thornton III, *Politics and Power in a Slave Society: Alabama, 1800–1860* (Baton Rouge, 1978); Eugene Genovese, *The Political Economy of Slavery* (New York, 1966); and Michael P. Johnson, *Toward a Patriarchal Republic: The Secession of Georgia* (Baton Rouge, 1977).

45. Tourgée grossly exaggerates the distinction between southern and northern immigrants as a source of sectional difference. *Cf.* Clement Eaton, *A History of the Old South* (2nd ed.; New York, 1966), Ch. 1; and Marcus L. Hanson, *The Atlantic Migration, 1670–1860* (New York, 1961). For some of the ramifications involved, see Edmund S. Morgan, *American Slavery, American Freedom: The Ordeal of Colonial Virginia* (New York, 1975), and Forrest McDonald and Grady McWhiney, "The Antebellum Southern Herdsman: A Reinterpretation," *Journal of Southern History,* XLI (1975), 147–66.

46. Tourgée's perception reflected his experiences in North Carolina and was more appropriate to the southeastern states than to the South as a whole. *Cf.* Wooster, *The People in Power* and *Politicians, Planters, and Plain Folk.*

47. In this testimony, Augustus R. Wright refers to being a Union man in the South just prior to secession.

48. Edward Hogan, "South Carolina Today," *International Review,* VIII (1880), 108–19.

49. Henry C. Dibble, *Why Reconstruction Failed. A Letter to the Vice-President of the United States from Henry C. Dibble of Louisiana* (New Orleans, 1877).

50. Former Confederate General Martin W. Gary was

considered the mastermind of a campaign of intimidation that carried the South Carolina elections of 1876 for the Democratic party. William A. Sheppard, *Red Shirts Remembered: Southern Brigadiers of the Reconstruction Period* (Atlanta, 1940), 46–50.

51. KKK Report, VII, 827. Since the 1940s, scholarship, by and large, sustains Tourgée's view of the so-called carpetbaggers, a term applied to any Republican. But Tourgée minimizes the role of carpetbaggers in some states, particularly in states with large black populations where it proved especially difficult to retain native white support. See Peter Kolchin, "Scalawags, Carpetbaggers, and Reconstruction: A Look at Southern Congressional Politics, 1868–1872," *Journal of Southern History*, XLV (1979), 63–76, and Current, *Those Terrible Carpetbaggers*.

52. Some scholars have emphasized the reality of this antebellum fear. See Steven A. Channing, *Crisis of Fear: Secession in South Carolina* (New York, 1970); George M. Fredrickson, *The Black Image in the White Mind: The Debate on Afro-American Character and Destiny, 1870–1914* (New York, 1971), 52–55.

53. One item of unusual general agreement found in the slave narrative collection edited by George P. Rawick is a memory of the always threatening presence of the "patterollers" in the slave South. Rawick (ed.), *The American Slave: A Composite Autobiography* (19 vols.; Westport, Conn., 1972), and *The American Slave: A Composite Autobiography, Supplement Series I* (12 vols.; Westport, Conn., 1977).

54. For contrasting analyses of the degrees of brutality and kindness in the slave system and resistance and accommodation to it, compare Aptheker, *American Negro Slave Revolts,* and Genovese, *Roll, Jordan, Roll.*

55. *The Statutes at Large of South Carolina, Edited Under Authority of the Legislature by David J. McCord, Volume 7 Containing the Acts Relating to Charleston, Courts, Slaves, and Rivers* (Columbia, S.C., 1840), 359–60. The opening page of this volume contains, however, the following disclaimer:

> As it is an age when our institutions are likely to be misrepresented, the Editor thinks it proper to call the attention of the reader to the fact that all the laws on the subject of slaves, from the year 1660 to 1751, included between the pages 343 and 426 of this volume, expired before the revolution. If the false philanthropist of the day chooses to quarrel with any enactments during that period, let him recollect that they were British, not American Laws; and that the free people of South Carolina have no cause to blush at any enactment of theirs.

In contrast, Howell Mendoes Henry, in *The Police Control of the Slave in South Carolina* (1914; rpr. New York, 1968), 190, states that "amended, of course, from time to time, the code of 1740 remained for one hundred and twenty years the organic slave law of the state."

56. The victim was James A. Patterson, a black member of the Mississippi Legislature, described by Albert T. Morgan as a cultivated and peace-loving man. Morgan, *Yazoo, or On the Picket Line of Freedom in the South. A Personal Narrative* (1884; rpr. New York, 1968), 482–84. Dixon was Henry M. Dixon. Further details of this entire incident may be found in Morgan, *Yazoo,* 479–84, 489–93.

57. According to Morgan's account, Dixon was shot down on the main street of Yazoo by a man named Barksdale, who Morgan believed was related to a prominent Mississippi family of that name. Morgan, *Yazoo,* 492.

58. "To secure the proper police of the country," the Confederate exemption act of October 11, 1862, exempted

one overseer for every plantation having as many as twenty slaves, or for any two plantations within five miles of each other with twenty slaves, or as specified by state law. As a concession to smaller plantations or perhaps to safety, the number was changed to fifteen slaves by the act of February 17, 1864. *The War of the Rebellion: A Compilation of the Official Records of the War of the Union and Confederate Armies* (130 vols.; Washington, D.C., 1880–1901), Ser. IV, Vol. II, 553, Vol. III, 180. These provisions have often been exaggerated to claim that the exemption was for every twenty or fifteen slaves. For example, see Paul D. Escott, *After Secession: Jefferson Davis and the Failure of Confederate Nationalism* (Baton Rouge, 1978), 120.

59. Hogan, "South Carolina Today," *International Review,* VIII (1880), 109–10.

60. Barnas Sears, a Baptist clergyman and educator, was general agent and principal leader of the Peabody Education Fund, which had been active in promoting southern education since shortly after the war. *Dictionary of American Biography,* XVI, 537–38.

# ERRATA

| PAGE NO. | LINE | CORRECTION |
|---|---|---|
| 28 | 10 | "Pond" should read "Pound." |
| 40 | 10 from the bottom | "1867" should read "1870." |
| 42 | 7 from the bottom | "Section 7" should be "Section 6." |
| 46 | 17 | "Calera" should be "Colera." |
| 47 | bottom line | "p. 419" should be "p. 418." |
| 49 | 12 from the bottom | "p. 849" should be "pp. 948–949." |
| 50 | 8 from the bottom | "p. 723" should be "pp. 722–723." |
| 51 | 15 from the bottom | "p. 574" should be "pp. 572, 574." |
| 59 | 7 | "p. 334" should be "p. 320." |
| 60 | 5 from the bottom | "pp. 114–115" should be "pp. 115–116." |

| | | |
|---|---|---|
| 61 | 14 from the bottom | Citation is from Vol. 6. |
| 64 | 15 | Citation is from Vol. 8. |
| 67 | 7 from the bottom | Citation is from Vol. 4. |
| 69 | 7 | "p. 1730" should be "p. 1738." |
| 72 | 14 from the bottom | "p. 828" should be "p. 838." |
| 74 | 14 | "The" should be "You." |
| 76 | 14 from the bottom | "p. 408" should be "pp. 338–339." |
| 76 | 12 from the bottom | "p. 433" should be "pp. 329–330, 335–336, 340." |
| 123 | 19 | Should read "debarred from Southern society;" |
| 129 | 2 from the bottom | "p. 958 *Reports*" should read "pp. 528–529." |
| 132 | 13 from the bottom | "p. 884" should be "p. 334." |
| 135 | 15 | "chap. vii" should be "chap. x." |